AUDIO ACCESS INCLUDED
Recorded Piano Accompaniments Online

PLAYBACK+
Speed • Pitch • Balance • Loop

SINGER'S JAZZ ANTHOLOGY | HIGH VOICE

george gershwin

Arranged by Brent Edstrom

4 BUT NOT FOR ME

9 EMBRACEABLE YOU

14 FASCINATING RHYTHM

24 A FOGGY DAY (IN LONDON TOWN)

28 HOW LONG HAS THIS BEEN GOING ON?

32 I GOT PLENTY O' NUTTIN'

19 I GOT RHYTHM

36 I LOVES YOU, PORGY

48 I'VE GOT A CRUSH ON YOU

43 ISN'T IT A PITY?

52 IT AIN'T NECESSARILY SO

57 LET'S CALL THE WHOLE THING OFF

62 LOVE IS HERE TO STAY

66 LOVE WALKED IN

76 THE MAN I LOVE

71 NICE WORK IF YOU CAN GET IT

80 OF THEE I SING

90 OH, LADY BE GOOD!

94 'S WONDERFUL

98 SOMEBODY LOVES ME

85 SOMEONE TO WATCH OVER M

102 SOON

106 SUMMERTIME

110 THEY ALL LAUGHED

115 THEY CAN'T TAKE THAT AWAY FROM ME

Cover photo © Getty Images / CBS Photo Archive / Contributor

To access audio visit:
www.halleonard.com/mylibrary

Enter Code
1969-4687-3605-1947

ISBN 978-1-5400-4196-8

Hal•Leonard®

Visit Hal Leonard Online at
www.halleonard.com

Contact us:
Hal Leonard
7777 West Bluemound Road
Milwaukee, WI 53213
Email: info@halleonard.com

In Europe, contact:
Hal Leonard Europe Limited
42 Wigmore Street
Marylebone, London, W1U 2RN
Email: info@halleonardeurope.com

In Australia, contact:
Hal Leonard Australia Pty. Ltd.
4 Lentara Court
Cheltenham, Victoria, 3192 Australia
Email: info@halleonard.com.au

ARRANGER'S NOTE

The vocalist's part in the *Singer's Jazz Anthology* matches the original sheet music but is *not* intended to be sung verbatim. Instead, melodic embellishments and alterations of rhythm and phrasing should be incorporated to both personalize a performance and conform to the accompaniments. In some cases, the form has been expanded to include "tags" and other endings not found in the original sheet music. In these instances, the term *ad lib.* indicates new melodic material appended to the original form.

Although the concept of personalizing rhythms and embellishing melodies might seem awkward to singers who specialize in classical music, there is a long tradition of melodic variation within the context of performance dating back to the Baroque. Not only do jazz singers personalize a given melody to fit the style of an accompaniment, they also develop a distinctive sound that helps *further* personalize their performances. Undoubtedly, the best strategy for learning how to stylize a jazz melody is to listen to recordings from the vocal jazz canon, including artists such as Nat King Cole, Ella Fitzgerald, Billie Holiday, Frank Sinatra, Sarah Vaughan, Nancy Wilson, and others.

The accompaniments in the *Singer's Jazz Anthology* can also be embellished by personalizing rhythms or dynamics, and chord labels are provided for pianists who are comfortable playing their own chord voicings. In some cases, optional, written-out improvisations are provided. These can be performed "as is," embellished, or skipped, depending on the performers' preference.

The included audio features piano recordings that can be used as a rehearsal aid or to accompany a performance. Tempi were selected to fit the character of each accompaniment, and the optional piano solos were omitted to provide a more seamless singing experience for vocalists who utilize them as backing tracks.

I hope you find many hours of enjoyment exploring the *Singer's Jazz Anthology* series!

Brent Edstrom

BUT NOT FOR ME

from GIRL CRAZY

Music and Lyrics by GEORGE GERSHWIN
and IRA GERSHWIN

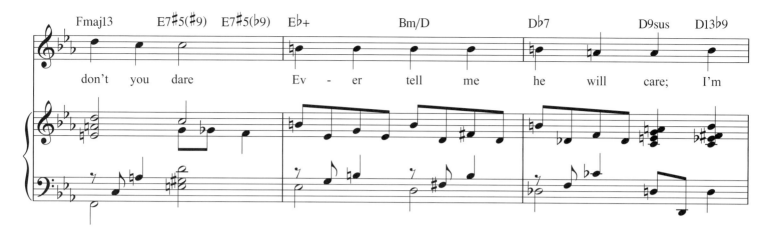

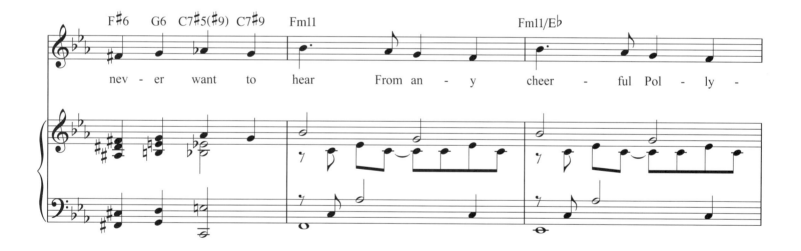

Moderately slow Swing *(smoothly)*

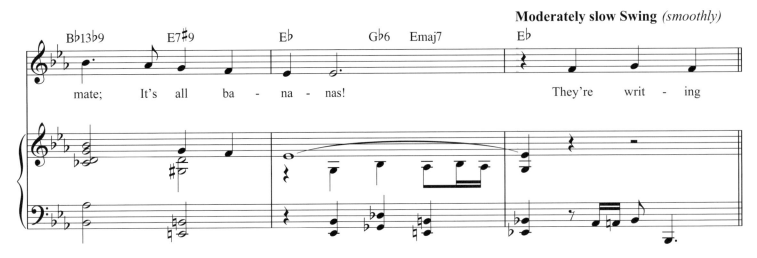

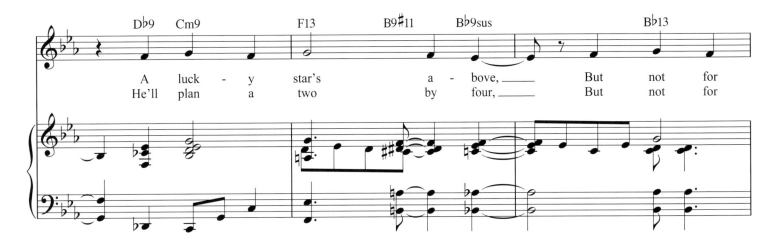

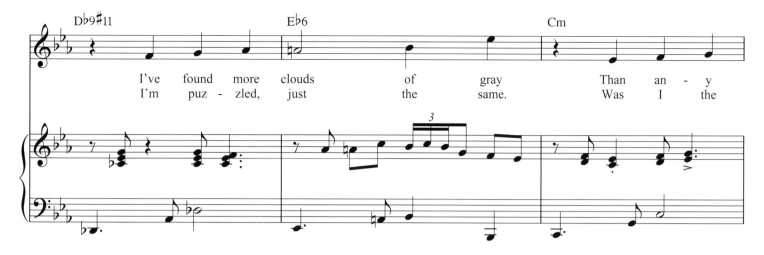

I've found more clouds of gray Than an - y
I'm puz - zled, just clouds of the same. Was I the

Rus - sian play Could guar - an - tee.
moth or flame? I'm all at sea.

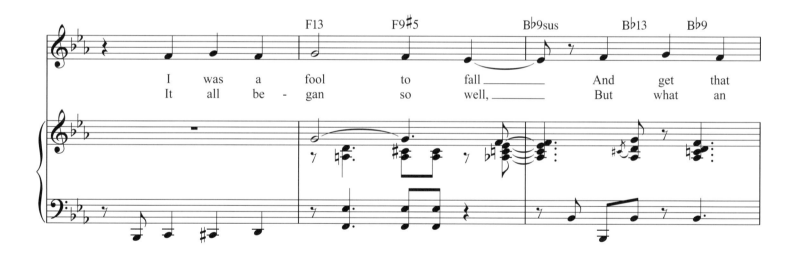

I was a fool to fall _____ And get that
It all be - gan so well, _____ But get what an

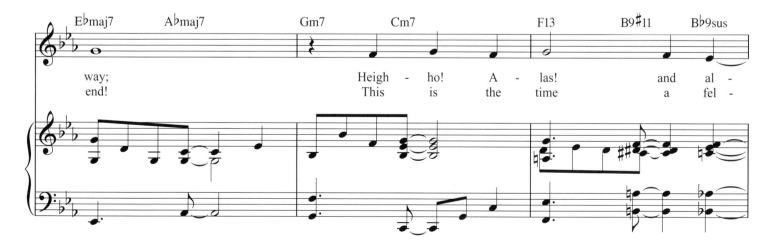

way; Heigh - ho! A - las! and al -
end! This is the time a fel -

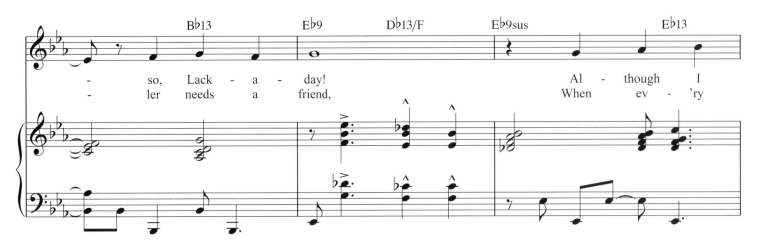

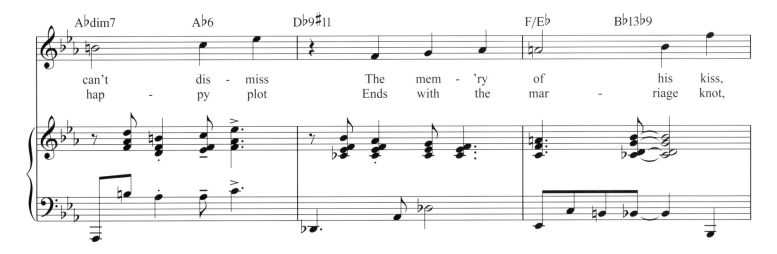

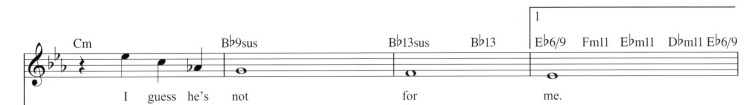

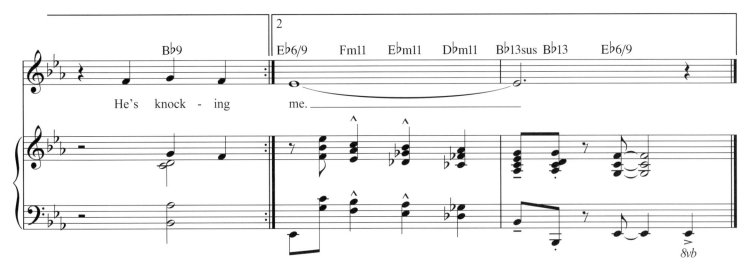

EMBRACEABLE YOU

from CRAZY FOR YOU

Music and Lyrics by GEORGE GERSHWIN
and IRA GERSHWIN

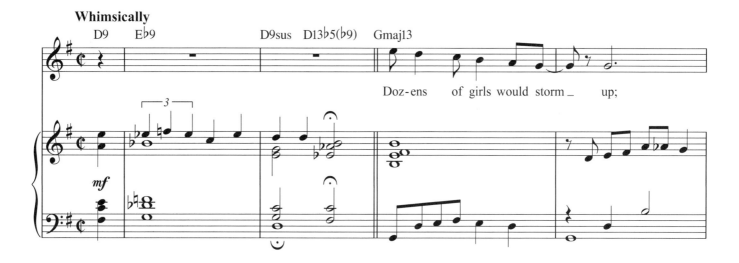

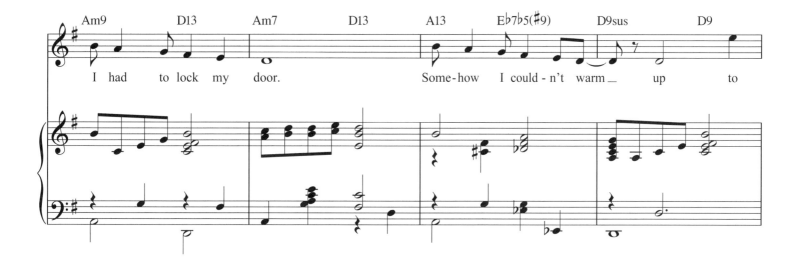

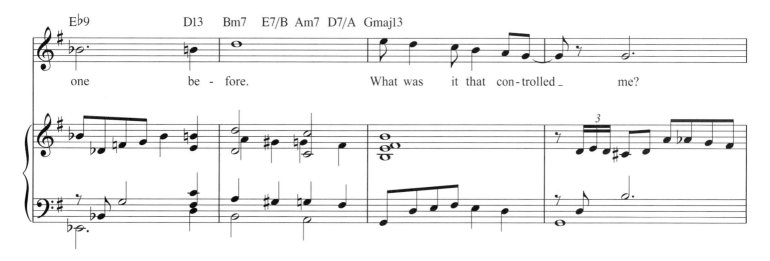

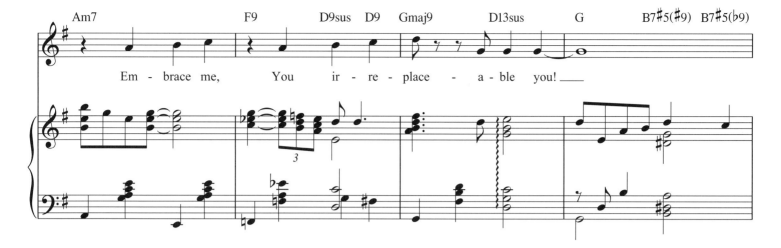

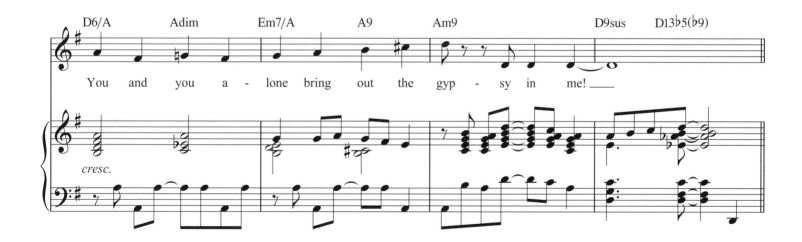

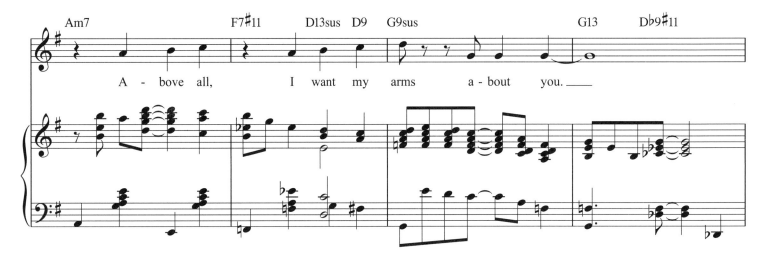

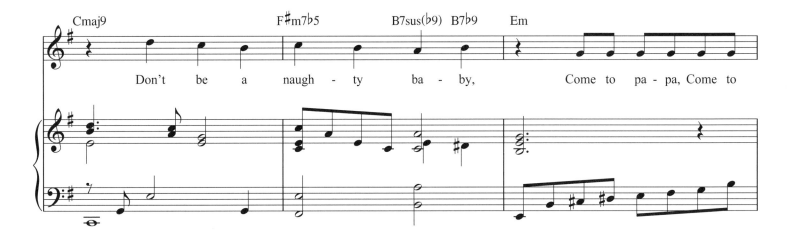

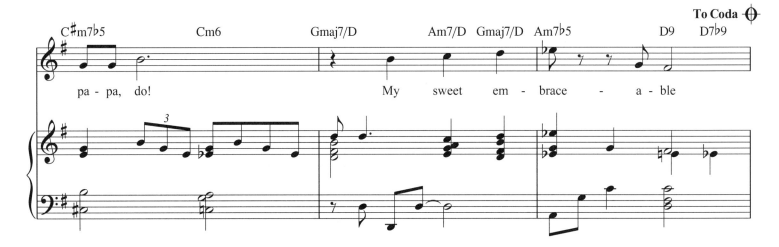

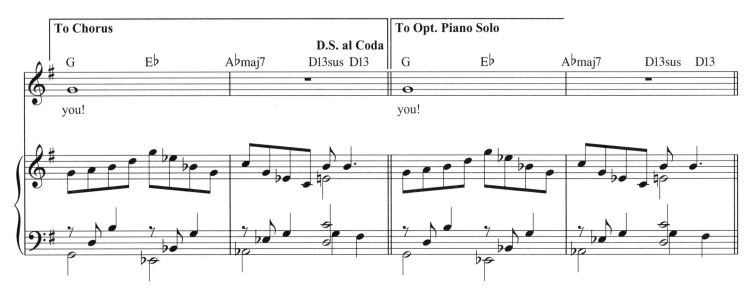

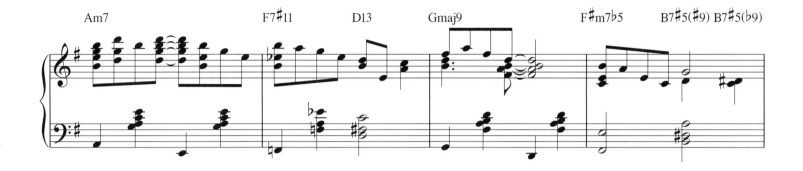

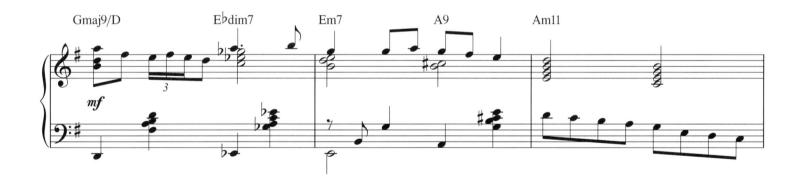

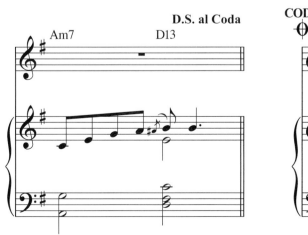

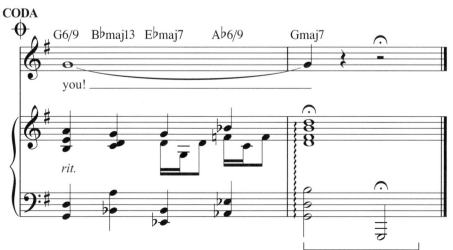

FASCINATING RHYTHM
from RHAPSODY IN BLUE

Music and Lyrics by GEORGE GERSHWIN
and IRA GERSHWIN

Moderately slow Swing

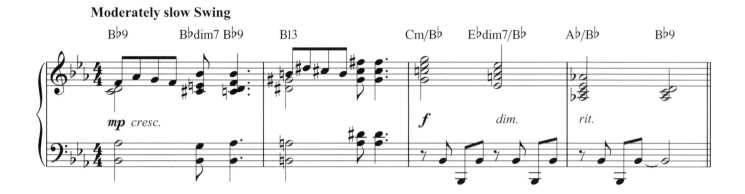

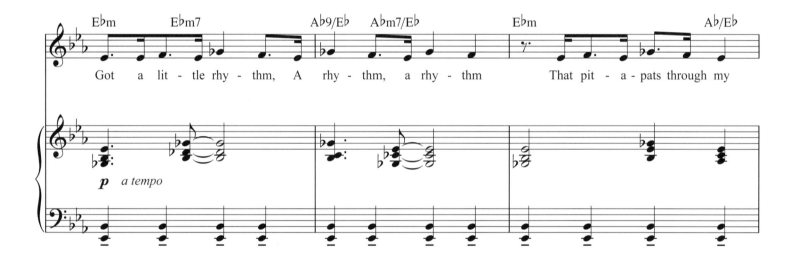

Got a lit-tle rhy-thm, A rhy-thm, a rhy-thm That pit-a-pats through my

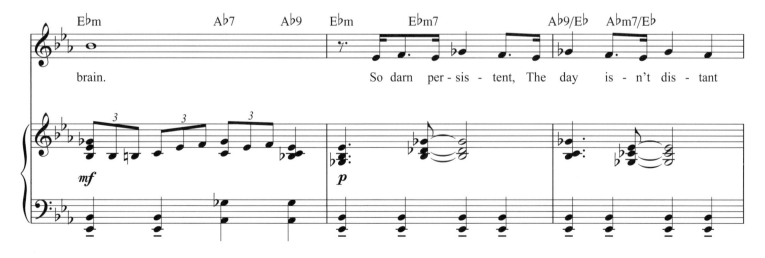

brain. So darn per-sis-tent, The day is-n't dis-tant

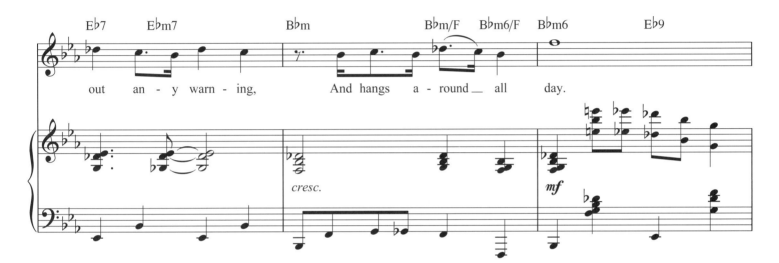

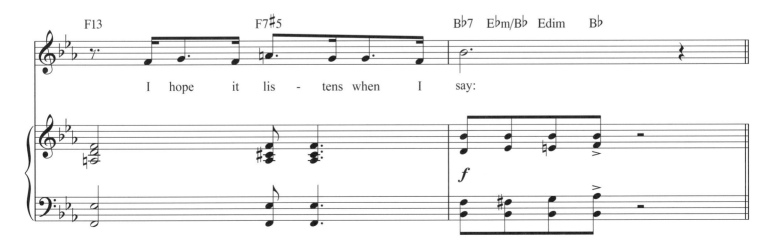

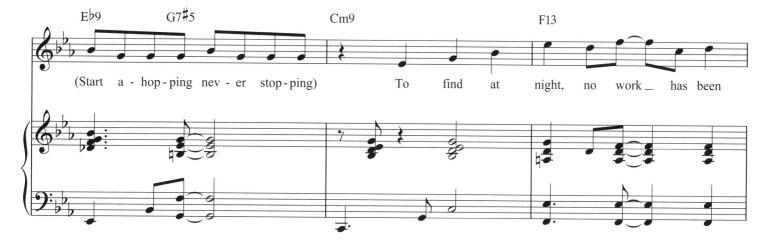

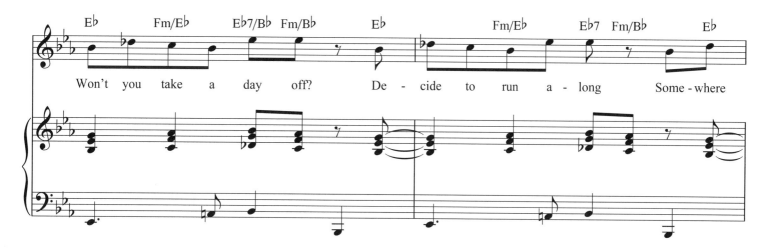

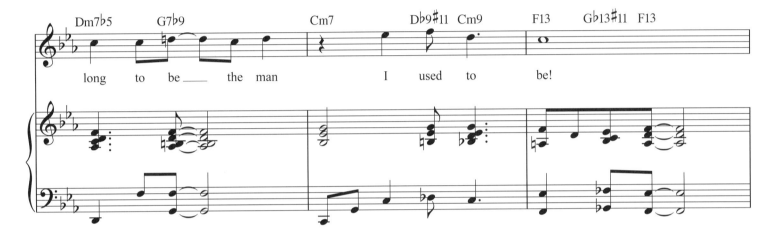

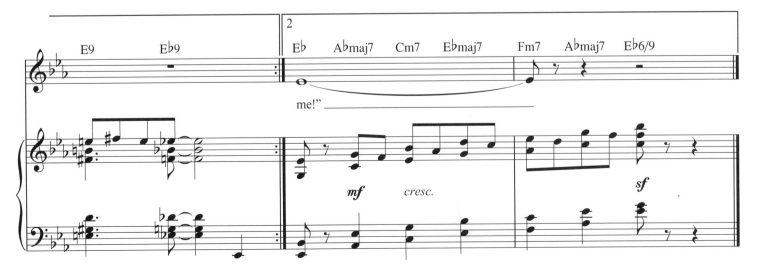

I GOT RHYTHM

from GIRL CRAZY

Music and Lyrics by GEORGE GERSHWIN
and IRA GERSHWIN

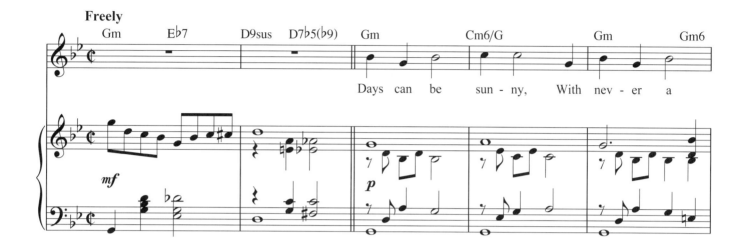

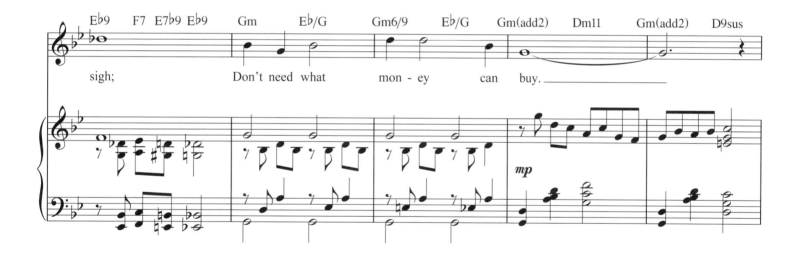

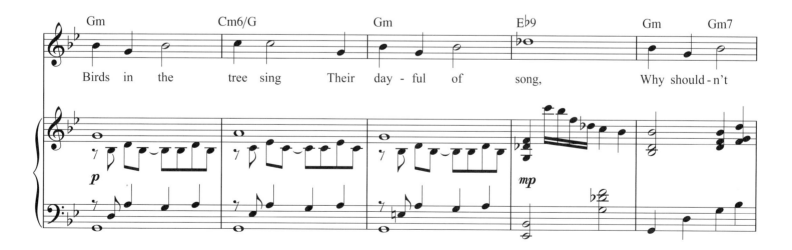

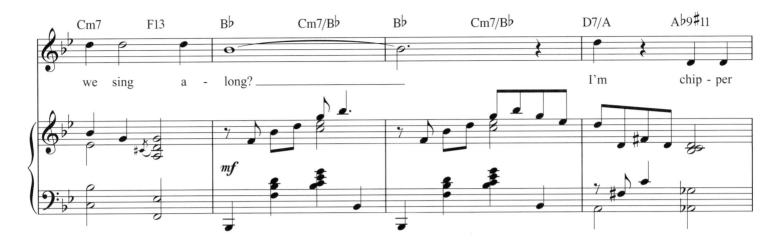

we sing a - long? _____ I'm chip - per

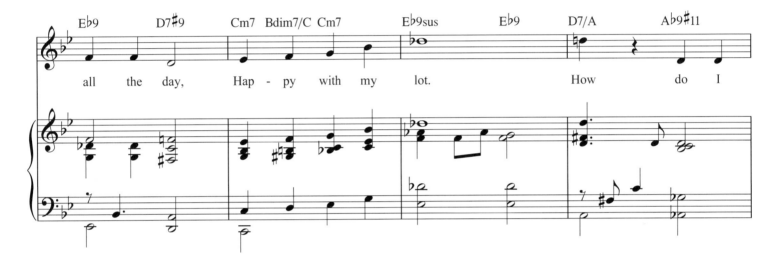

all the day, Hap - py with my lot. How do I

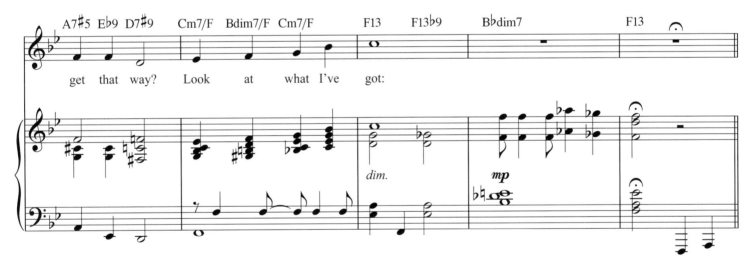

get that way? Look at what I've got:

Moderate Swing

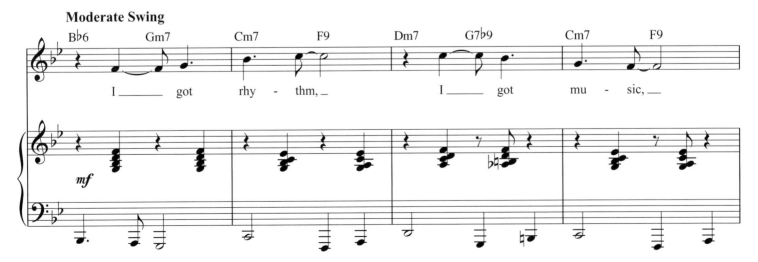

I _____ got rhy - thm, ___ I _____ got mu - sic, ___

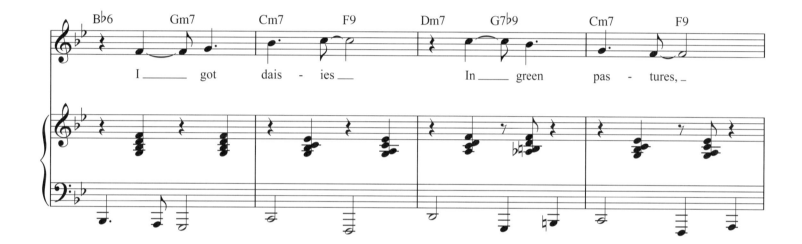

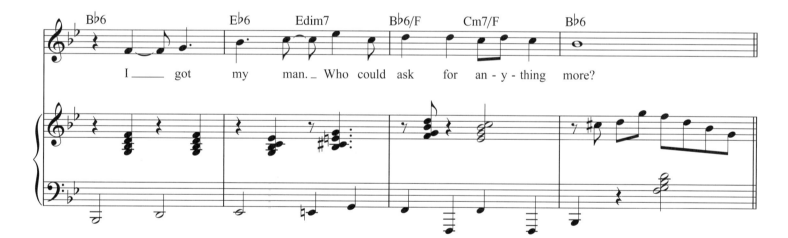

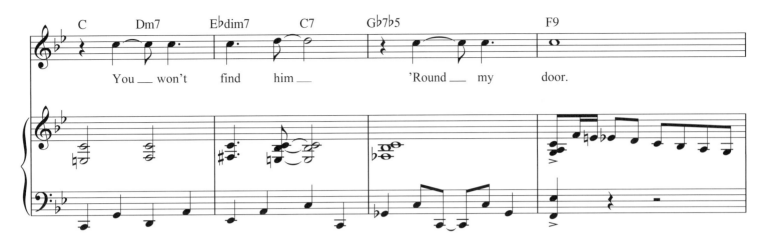

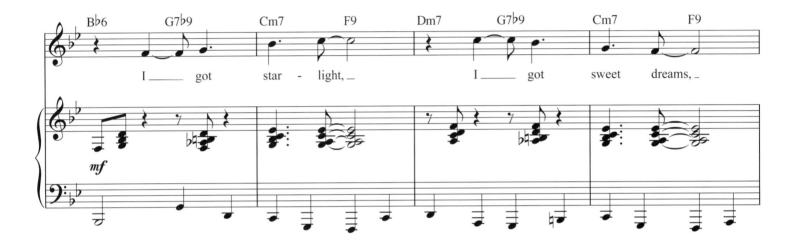

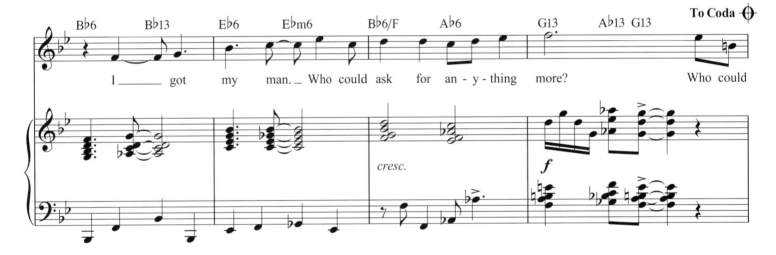

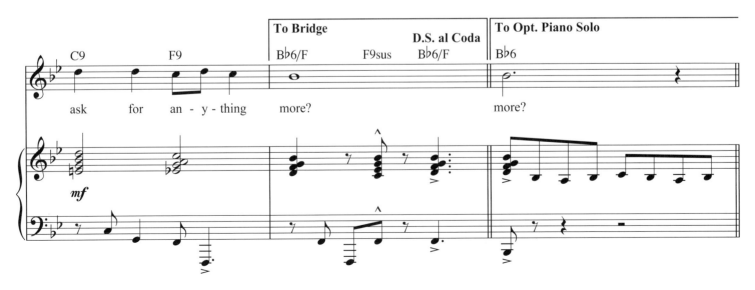

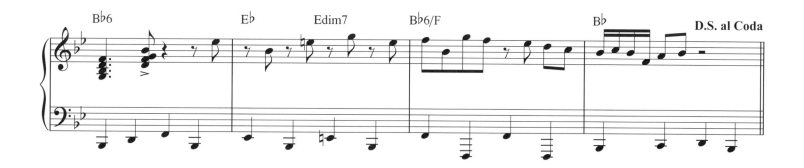

CODA

ask for an - y - thing more? _____

A FOGGY DAY
(In London Town)
from A DAMSEL IN DISTRESS

Music and Lyrics by GEORGE GERSHWIN
and IRA GERSHWIN

blue. _____ But as I walked through the fog - gy streets a - lone, It

Moderate Swing

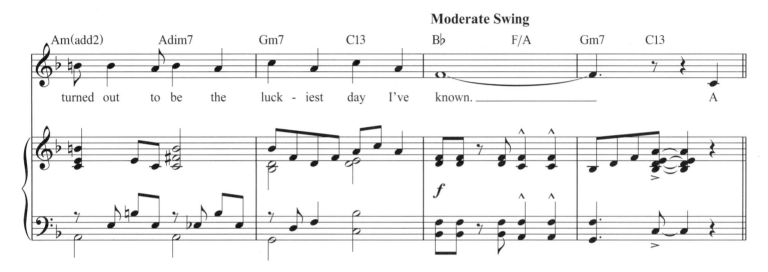

turned out to be the luck - iest day I've known. _____ A

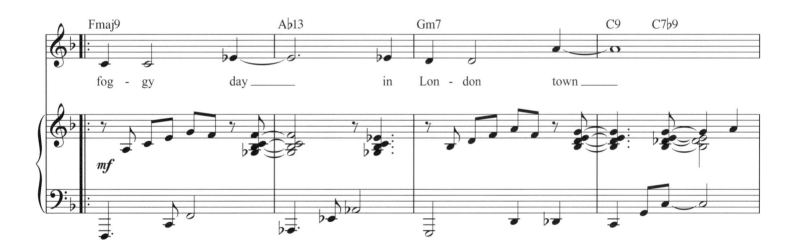

fog - gy day _____ in Lon - don town _____

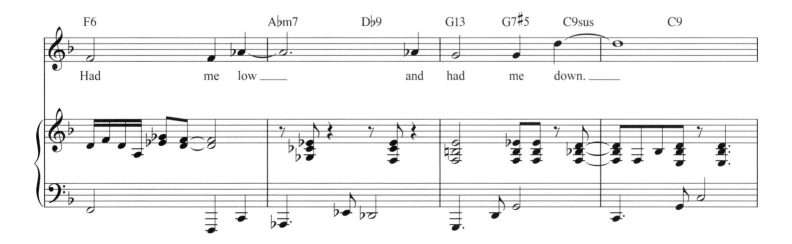

Had me low _____ and had me down. _____

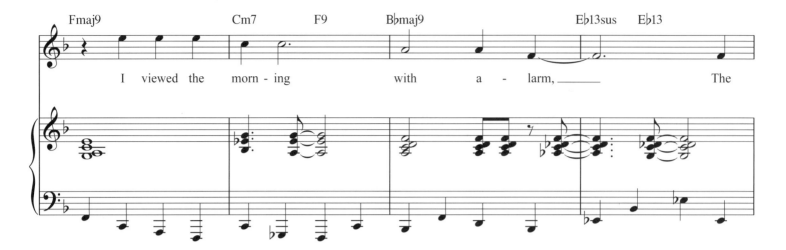

I viewed the morn - ing with a - larm, _____ The

Brit - ish Mu - se - um had lost its charm. _____ How

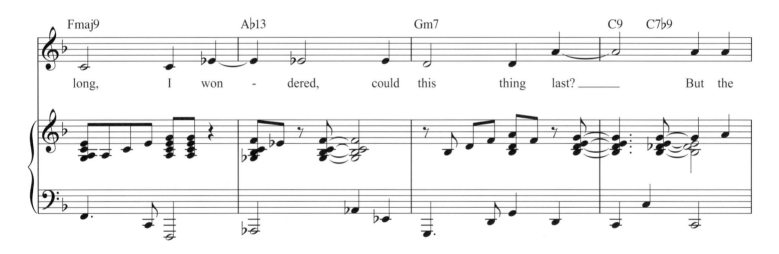

long, I won - dered, could this thing last? _____ But the

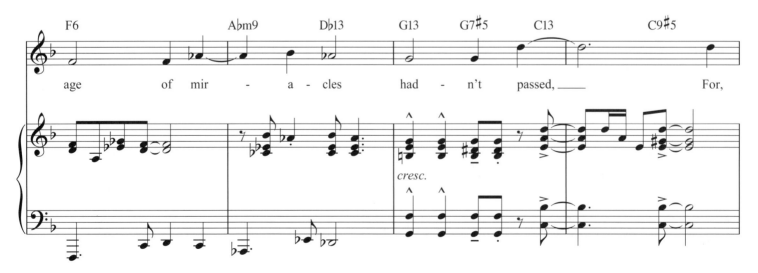

age of mir - a - cles had - n't passed, _____ For,

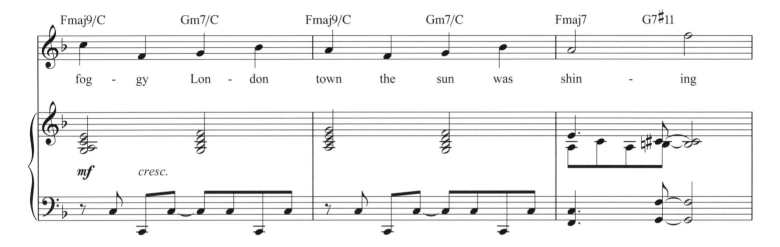

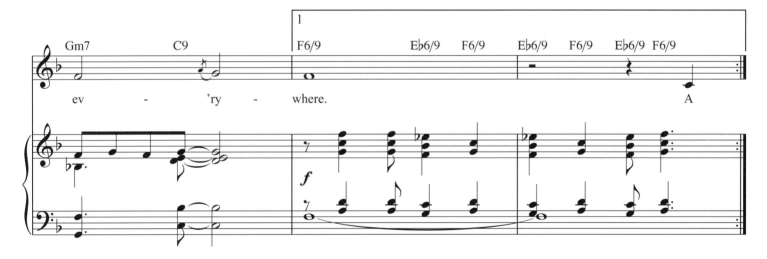

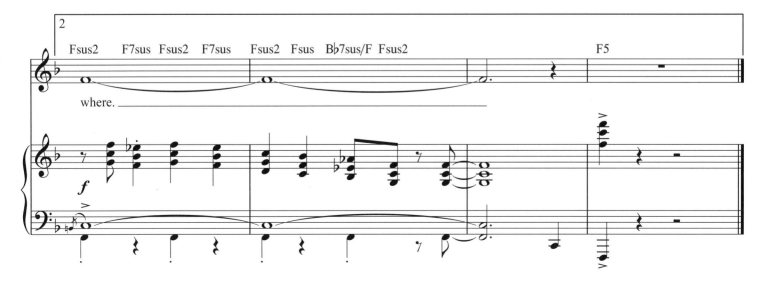

HOW LONG HAS THIS BEEN GOING ON?

from ROSALIE

Music and Lyrics by GEORGE GERSHWIN
and IRA GERSHWIN

Lit - tle wow, _ tell me now. _ How long has this been go - ing on? _
Lis - ten, you, _ tell me, do. _ How long has this been go - ing on? _

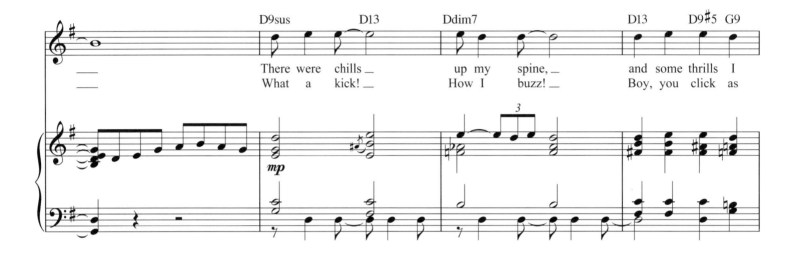

_ There were chills _ up my spine, _ and some thrills I
_ What a kick! _ How I buzz! _ Boy, you click as

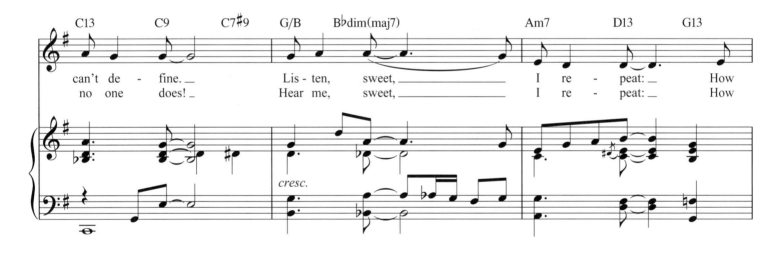

can't de - fine. _ Lis - ten, sweet, _____ I re - peat: _ How
no one does! _ Hear me, sweet, _____ I re - peat: _ How

long has this been go - ing on? _ Oh, I feel that I could melt; _
long has this been go - ing on? _ Dear, when in your arms I creep, _

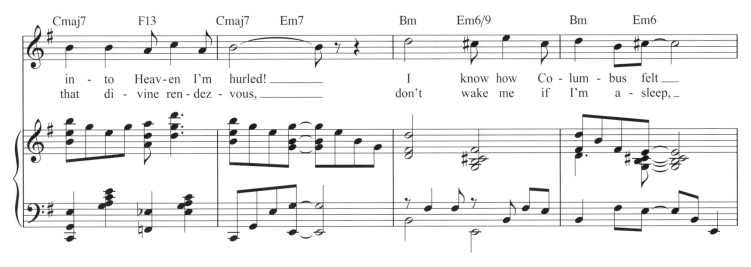

in - to Heav - en I'm hurled! _____ I know how Co - lum - bus felt __
that di - vine ren - dez - vous, _____ don't wake me if I'm a - sleep, __

find - ing an - oth - er world! Kiss me once, __ then once more; __
let me dream that it's true. Kiss me twice, __ then once more; __

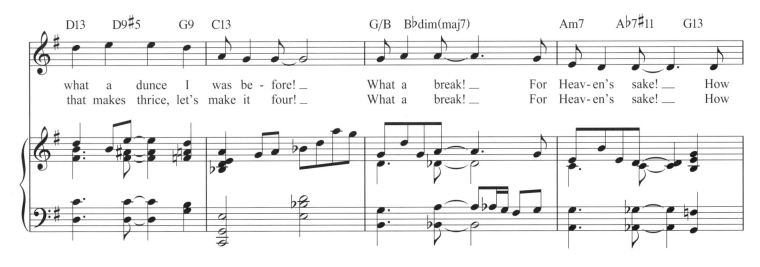

what a dunce I was be - fore! __ What a break! __ For Heav - en's sake! __ How
that makes thrice, let's make it four! __ What a break! __ For Heav - en's sake! __ How

long has this been go - ing on? ___
long has this been go - ing on? __

I GOT PLENTY O' NUTTIN'

from PORGY AND BESS®

Music and Lyrics by GEORGE GERSHWIN,
DuBOSE and DOROTHY HEYWARD
and IRA GERSHWIN

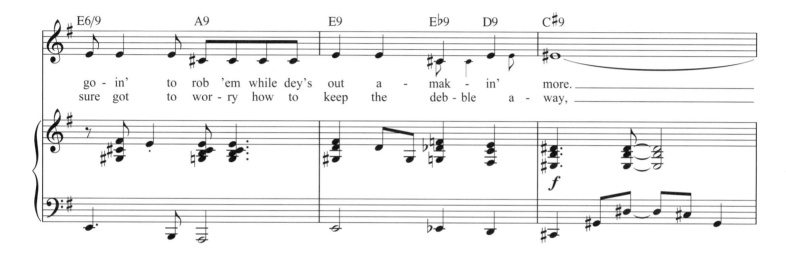

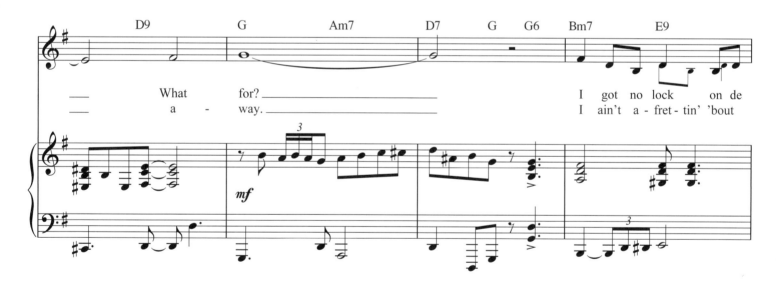

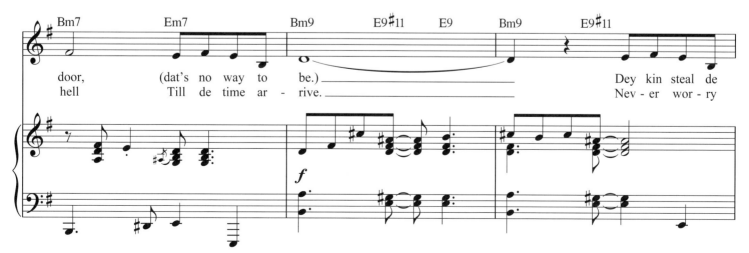

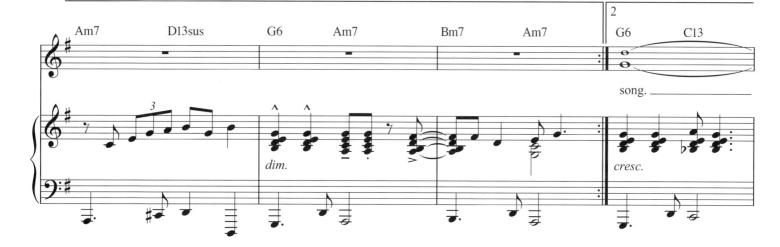

I LOVES YOU, PORGY

from PORGY AND BESS®

Music and Lyrics by GEORGE GERSHWIN,
DuBOSE and DOROTHY HEYWARD
and IRA GERSHWIN

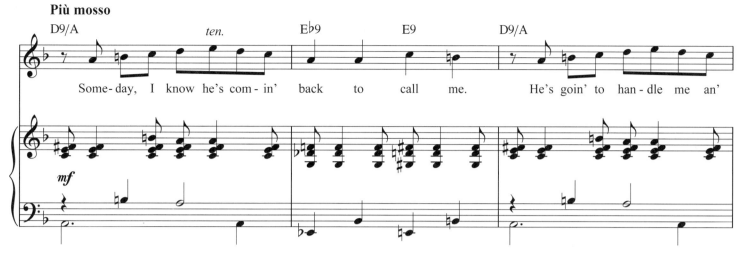

Some-day, I know he's com-in' back to call me. He's goin' to han-dle me an'

hol' me so. It's goin' to be like dy-in', Por-gy, deep in-side me.

But when he calls, I know I have to go.

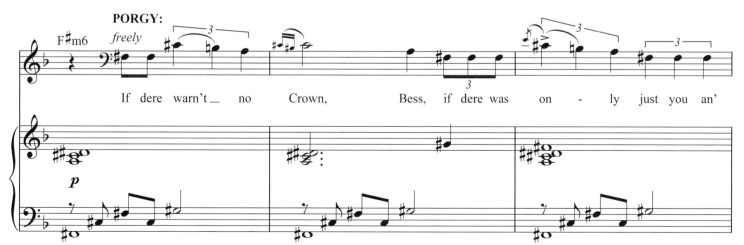

PORGY:

If dere warn't no Crown, Bess, if dere was on-ly just you an'

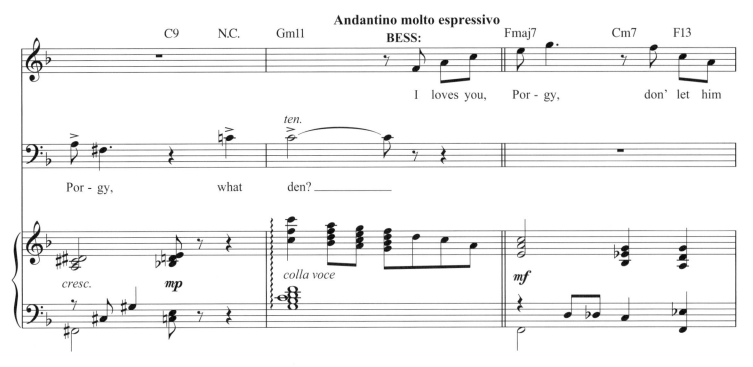

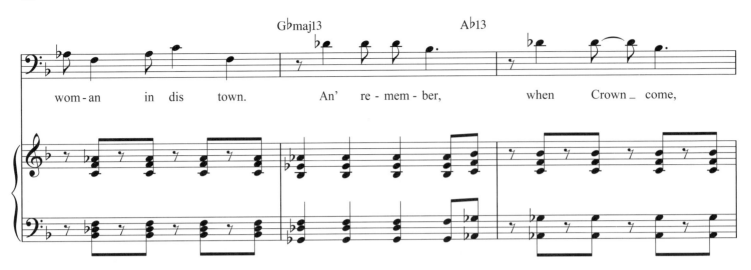

wom-an in dis town. An' re-mem-ber, when Crown come,

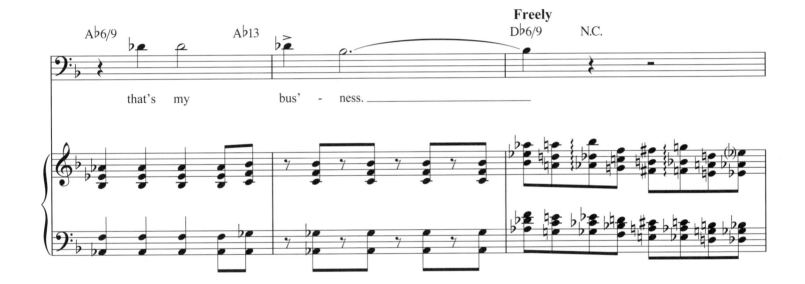

that's my bus'-ness.

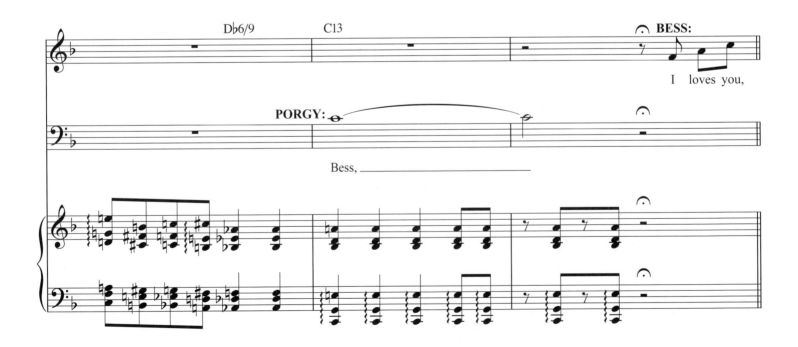

PORGY: Bess,

BESS: I loves you,

I wants to stay here _____ wid you for-
can't you un-der-stan'? You go-in' to go a-bout yo' bus'-ness sing-in',

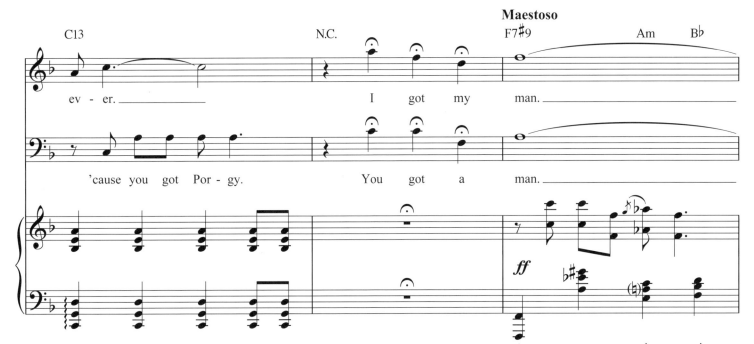

ev - er. _____ I got my man. _____
'cause you got Por - gy. You got a man. _____

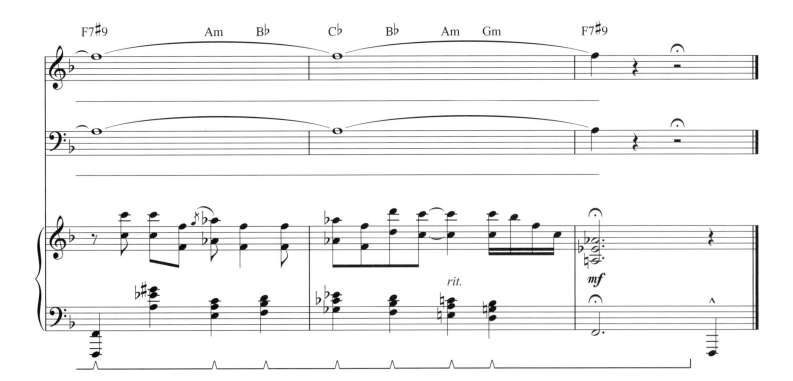

ISN'T IT A PITY?

from PARDON MY ENGLISH

Music and Lyrics by GEORGE GERSHWIN
and IRA GERSHWIN

Moderate Swing

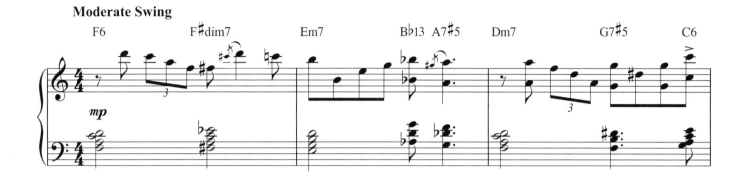

Michael: Why did I wan - der here and there and yon - der,
Ilse: While you were flit - ting I was bus - y knit - ting,

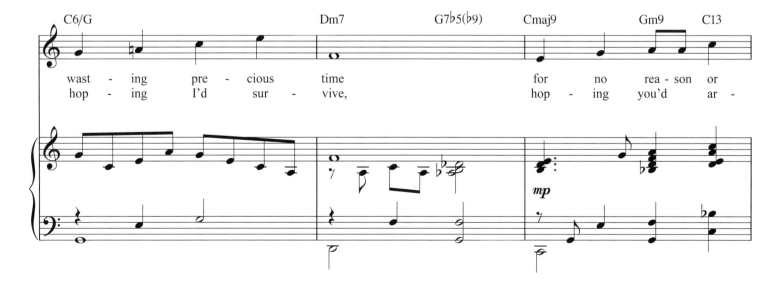

wast - ing pre - cious time for no rea - son or
hop - ing I'd sur - vive, hop - ing you'd ar -

Moderately slow Swing, with expression

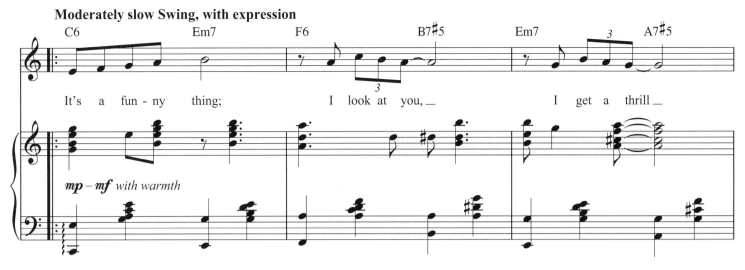

It's a fun-ny thing; I look at you, __ I get a thrill __

I nev-er knew. __ Is-n't it a pit-y we nev-er met __ be -

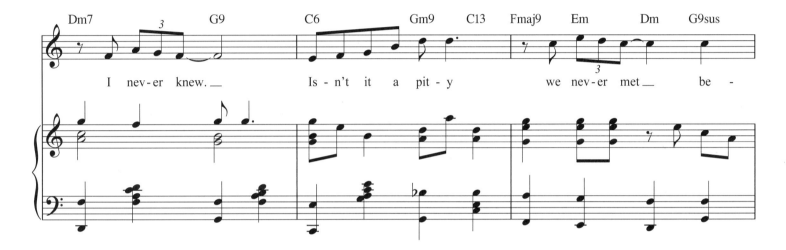

fore? Here we are at last!

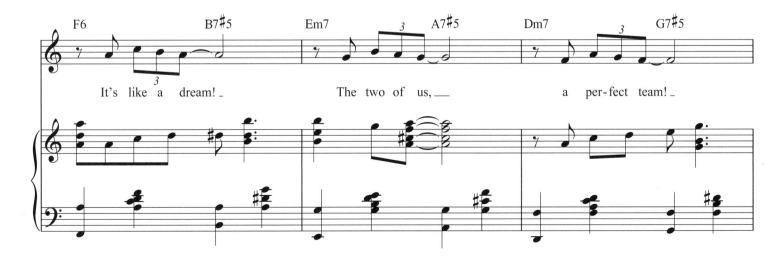

It's like a dream! _ The two of us, __ a per-fect team! _

Hap - pi - est of men I'm sure to be, ___ if on - ly you ___
Let's for - get the past, let's both a - gree ___ that I'm for you ___

will say to me, ___ "It's an aw - ful pit - y we nev - er, nev - er met be -
and you're for me, ___ and it's such a pit - y we nev - er, nev - er met be -

fore."   fore. ___

I'VE GOT A CRUSH ON YOU

from STRIKE UP THE BAND

Music and Lyrics by GEORGE GERSHWIN
and IRA GERSHWIN

Light, playful Swing

He: How
She: How

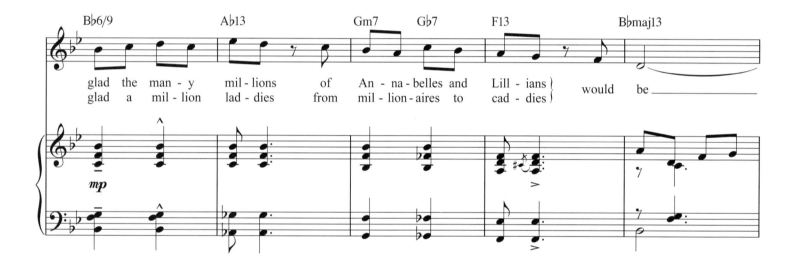

glad the man - y mil - lions of An - na - belles and Lill - ians
glad a mil - lion lad - dies from mil - lion - aires to cad - dies would be _____

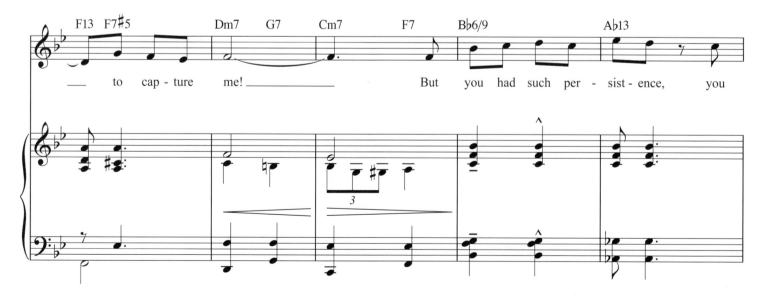

_____ to cap - ture me! _____ But you had such per - sist - ence, you

Relaxed Swing, not too fast

view. _____ I've got a crush on you, _____ sweet - ie pie, _____

_____ All the day and night - time hear me sigh. _____ { I
                                                          { This

nev - er had _____ the least no - tion _____ that I could fall with _____
is - n't just _____ a flir - ta - tion; _____ we're prov - ing that there's _____

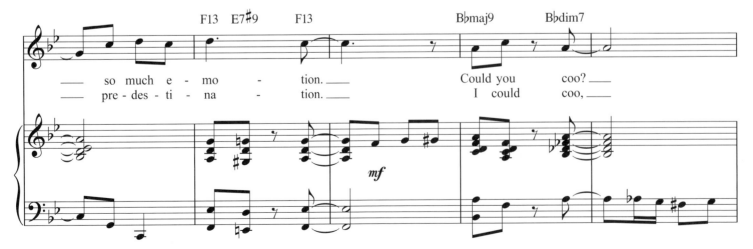

_____ so much e - mo - tion. _____ Could you coo? _____
_____ pre - des - ti - na - tion. _____ I could coo, _____

Could you   care ___   for a   cun - ning   cot - tage
I   could   care ___   for that   cun - ning   cot - tage

we   could   share? ___   The   world   will   par - don   my
we   could   share. ___   Your   mush   I   nev - er   shall

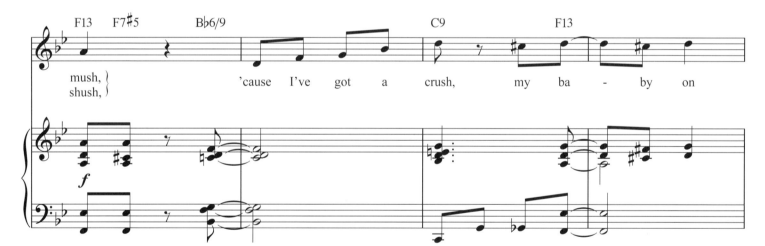

mush, }   'cause I've got a   crush,   my   ba - by   on
shush, }

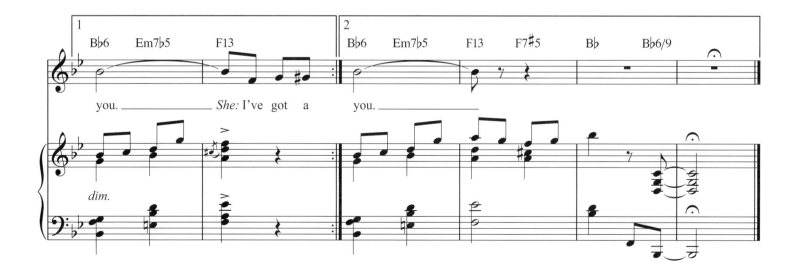

you. _____   *She:* I've got a   you. _____

IT AIN'T NECESSARILY SO

from PORGY AND BESS®

Music and Lyrics by GEORGE GERSHWIN,
DuBOSE and DOROTHY HEYWARD
and IRA GERSHWIN

Moderate Swing, with humor

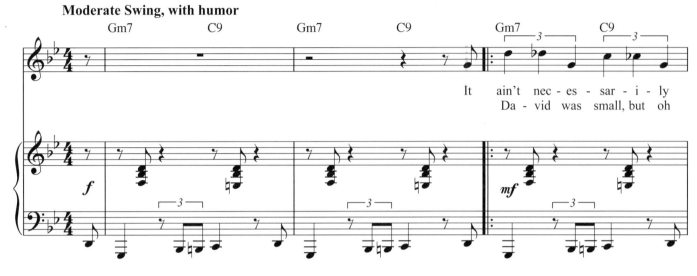

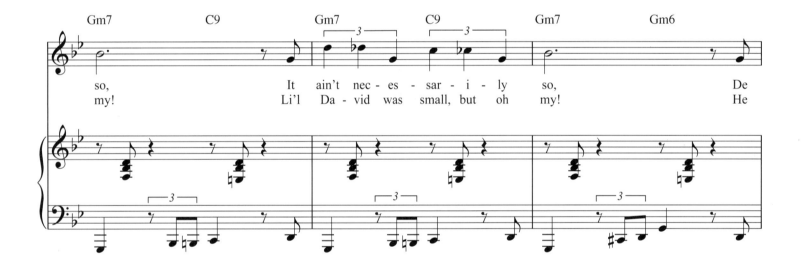

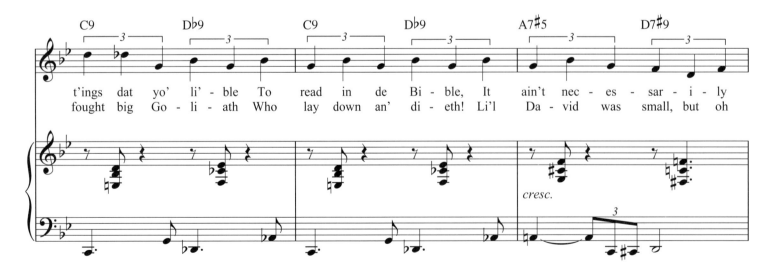

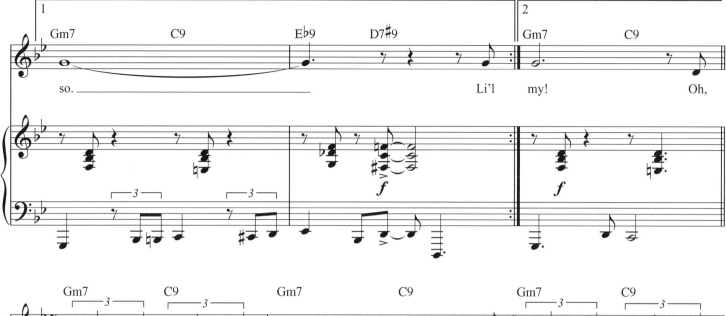

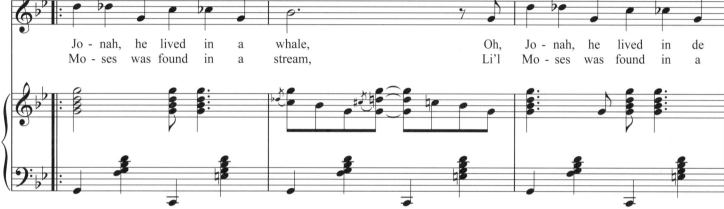

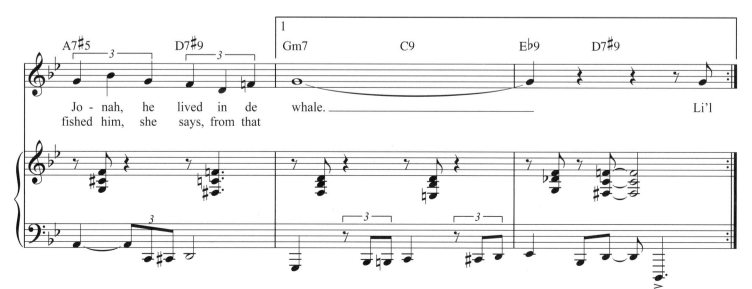

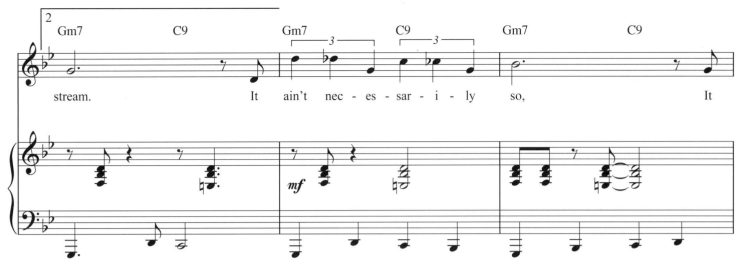

stream. It ain't nec - es - sar - i - ly so, It

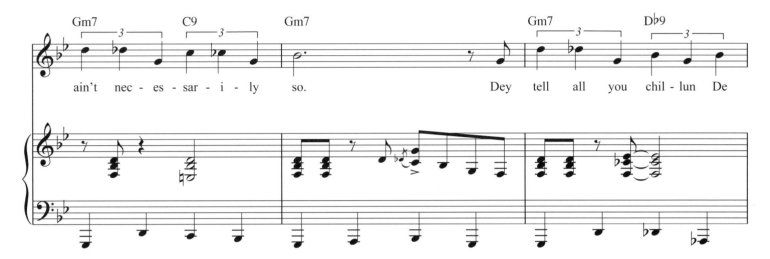

ain't nec - es - sar - i - ly so. Dey tell all you chil - lun De

deb - ble's a vil - lun, But 'tain't nec - es - sar - i - ly so. _____ To

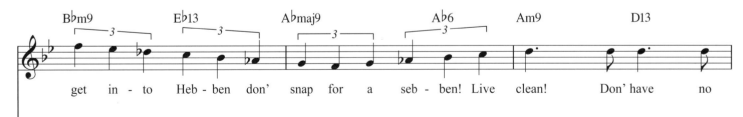

get in - to Heb - ben don' snap for a seb - ben! Live clean! Don' have no

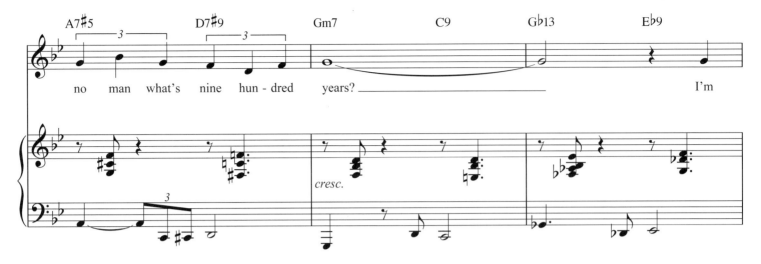

no man what's nine hun-dred years? _____ I'm

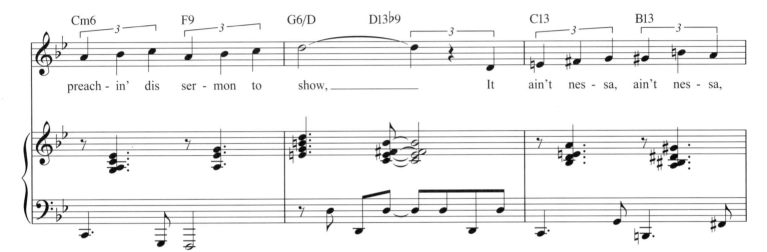

preach-in' dis ser-mon to show, _____ It ain't nes-sa, ain't nes-sa,

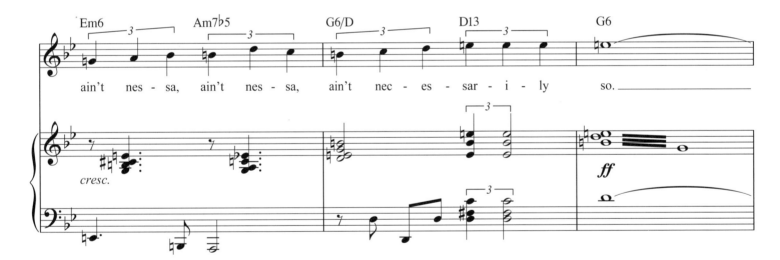

ain't nes-sa, ain't nes-sa, ain't nec-es-sar-i-ly so. _____

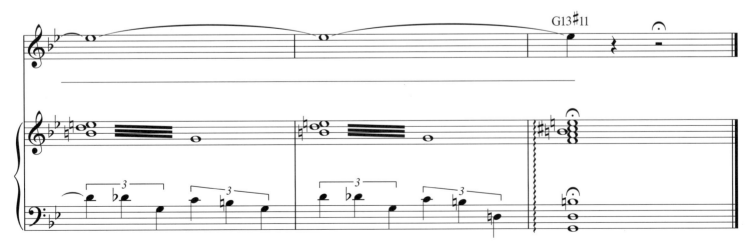

LET'S CALL THE WHOLE THING OFF
from SHALL WE DANCE

Music and Lyrics by GEORGE GERSHWIN
and IRA GERSHWIN

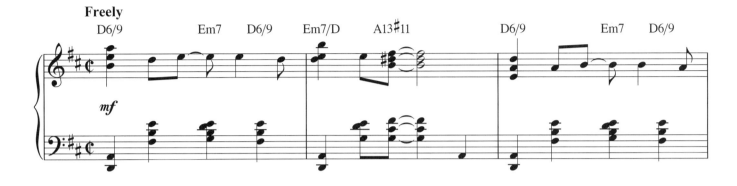

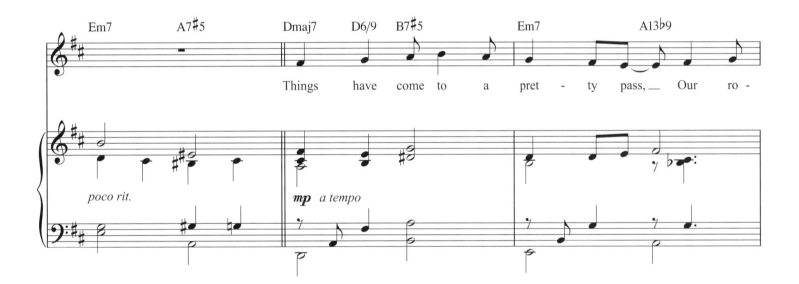

Things have come to a pret-ty pass,— Our ro-

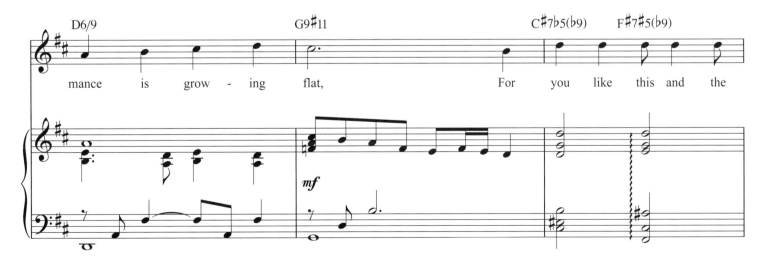

mance is grow-ing flat, For you like this and the

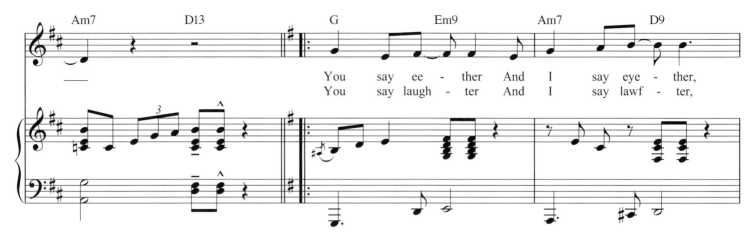

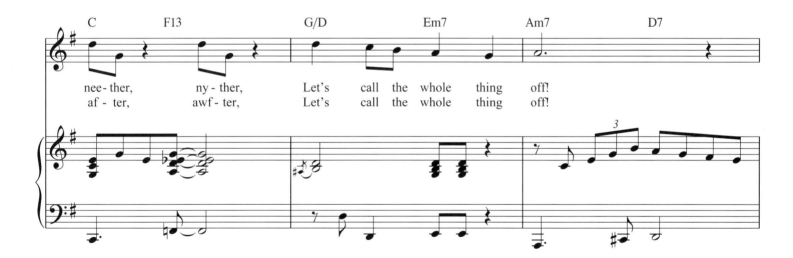

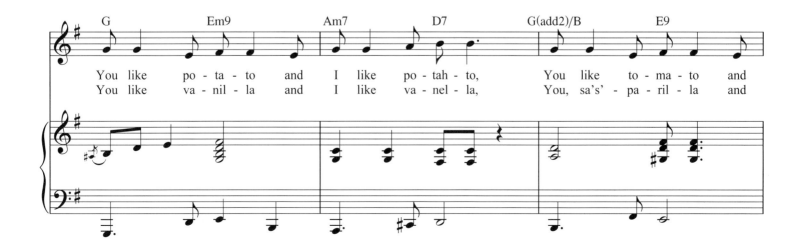

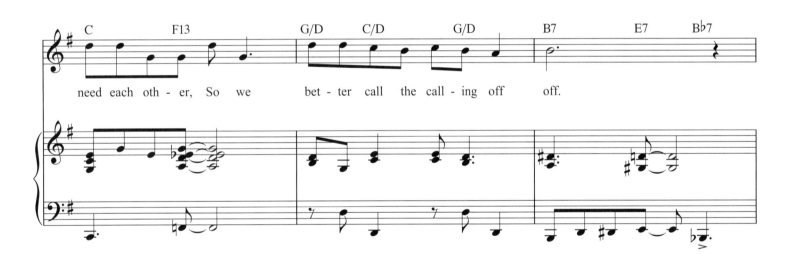

LOVE IS HERE TO STAY
from GOLDWYN FOLLIES

Music and Lyrics by GEORGE GERSHWIN
and IRA GERSHWIN

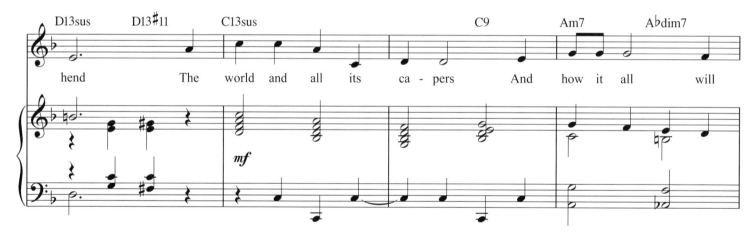

The more I read the pa-pers The less I com-pre-

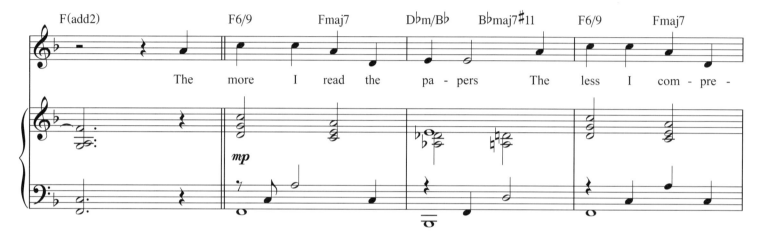

hend The world and all its ca-pers And how it all will

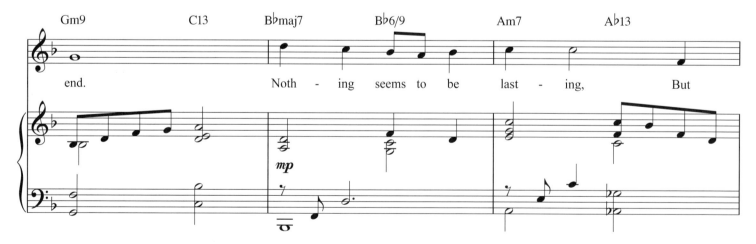

end. Noth-ing seems to be last-ing, But

go-ing a long, long way. In time the Rock-ies may crum-ble, Gi-

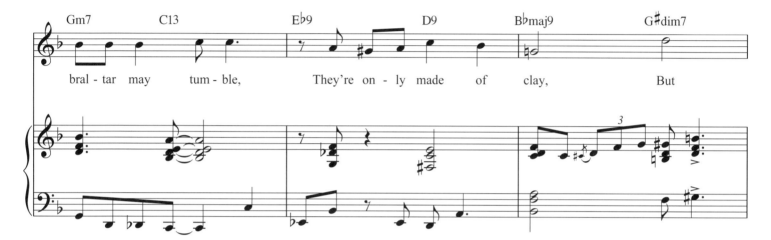

bral-tar may tum-ble, They're on-ly made of clay, But

our love is here to stay.

It's ver-y stay.

LOVE WALKED IN
from GOLDWYN FOLLIES

Music and Lyrics by GEORGE GERSHWIN
and IRA GERSHWIN

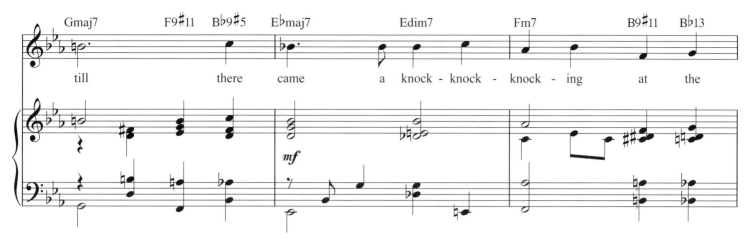

till there came a knock-knock-knock-ing at the

Moderately slow Swing

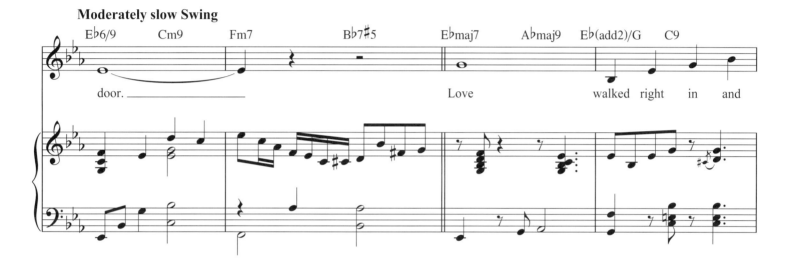

door. _____ Love walked right in and

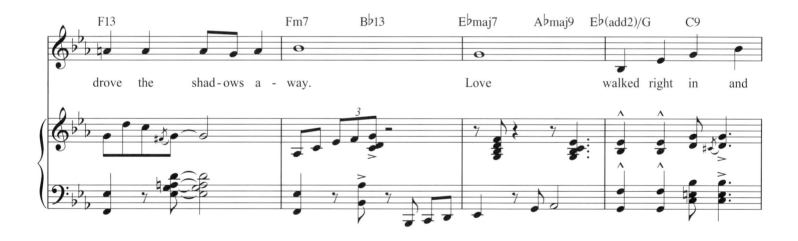

drove the shad-ows a - way. Love walked right in and

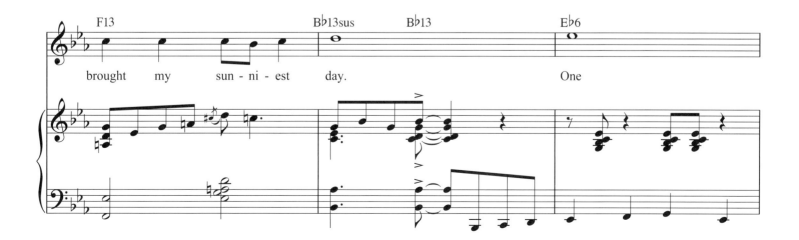

brought my sun-ni-est day. One

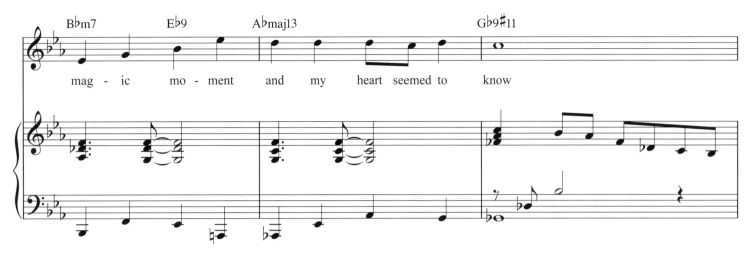

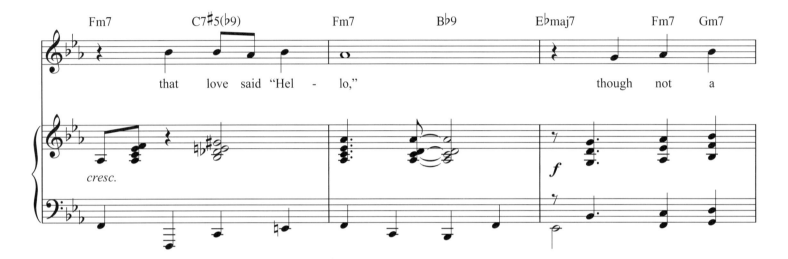

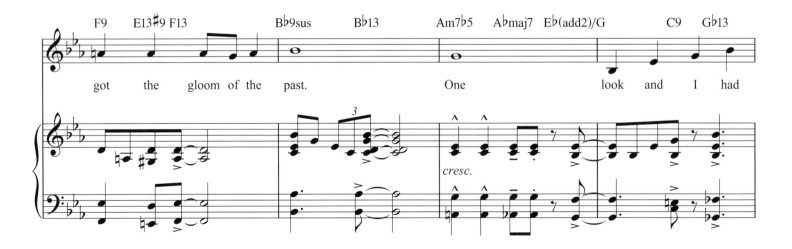

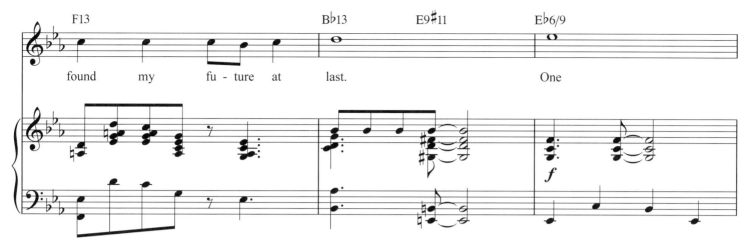

found my fu-ture at last. One

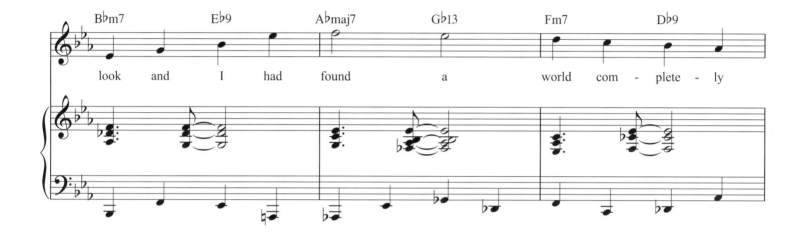

look and I had found a world com-plete-ly

To Coda ⊕ | **To 2nd Verse**

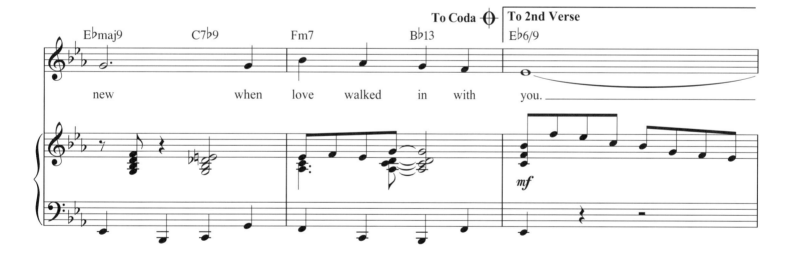

new when love walked in with you.

D.S. al Coda | **To Opt. Piano Solo**

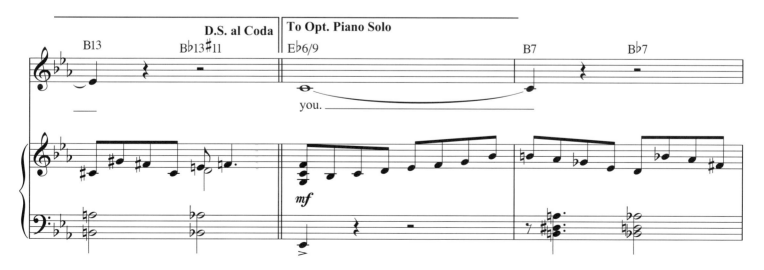

you.

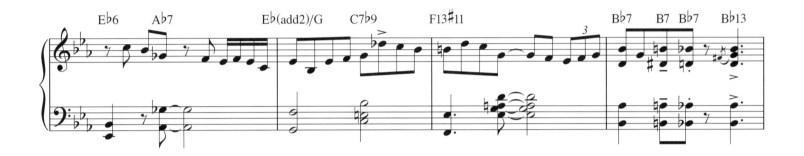

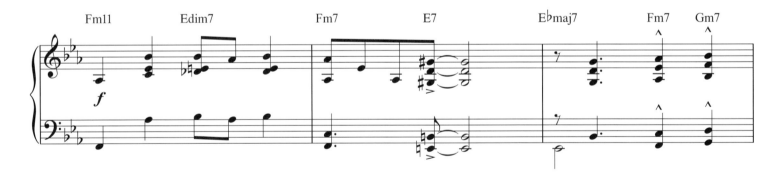

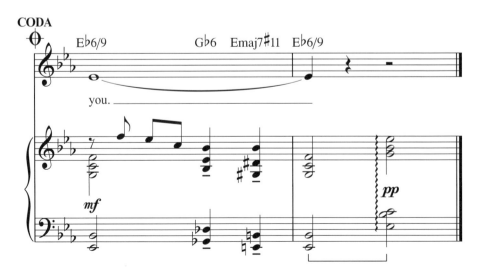

NICE WORK IF YOU CAN GET IT

from A DAMSEL IN DISTRESS

Music and Lyrics by GEORGE GERSHWIN
and IRA GERSHWIN

name. The fact is, the on - ly work that real - ly

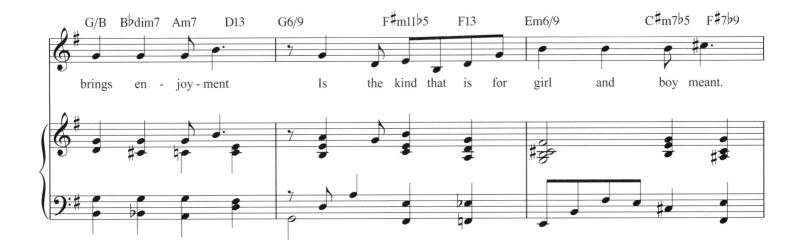

brings en - joy - ment Is the kind that is for girl and boy meant.

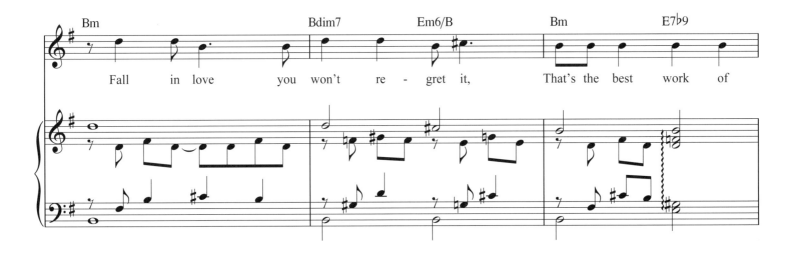

Fall in love you won't re - gret it, That's the best work of

Moderate Swing

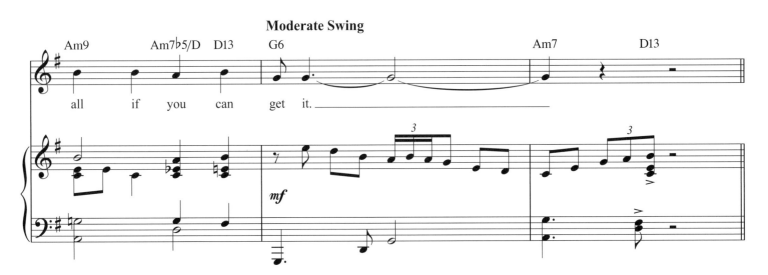

all if you can get it.

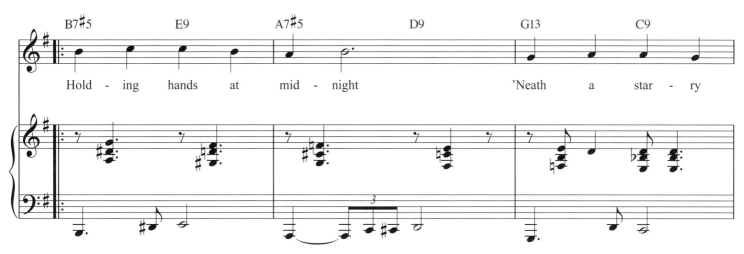

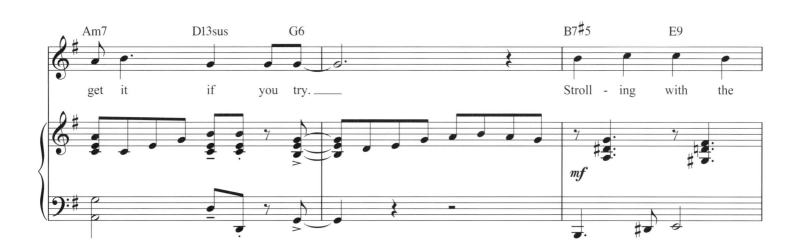

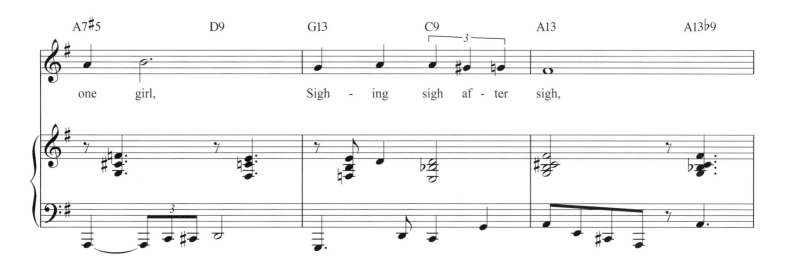

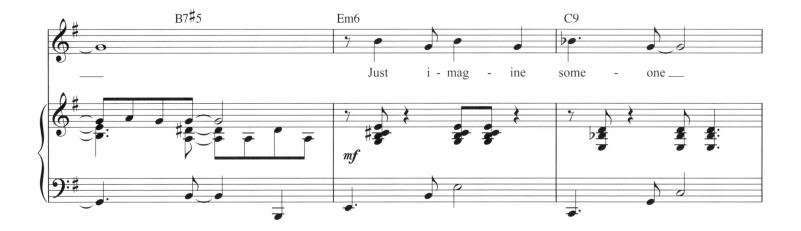

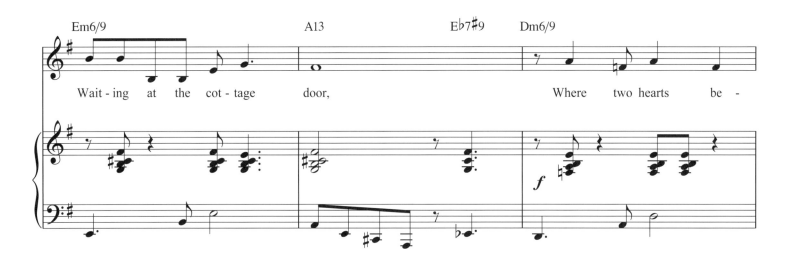

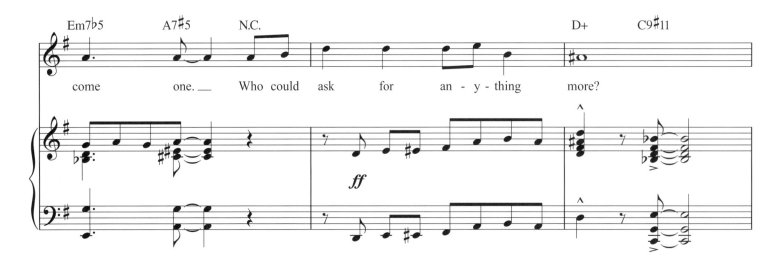

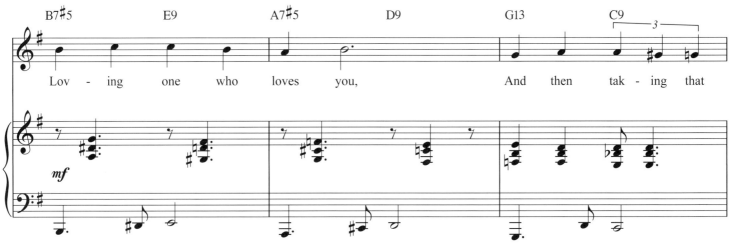

Lov - ing one who loves you, And then tak - ing that

vow, Nice work __ if you can get it, And if you

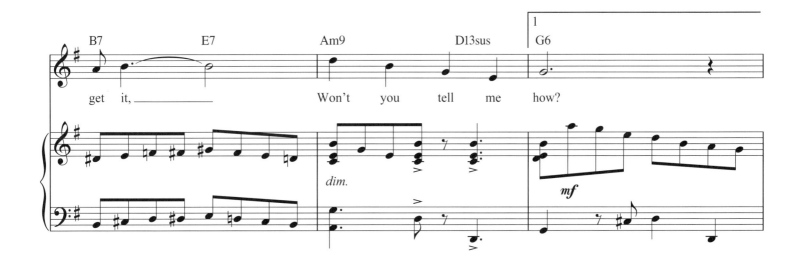

get it, _____ Won't you tell me how?

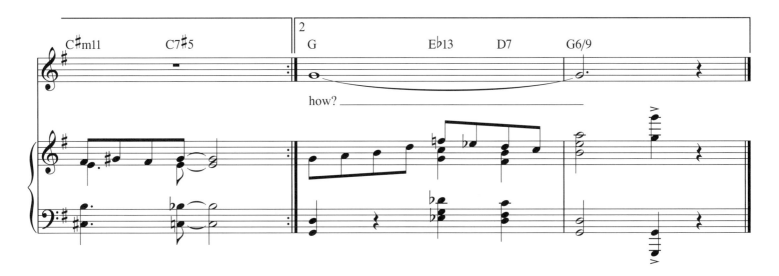

how? _____

THE MAN I LOVE

from LADY BE GOOD

Music and Lyrics by GEORGE GERSHWIN
and IRA GERSHWIN

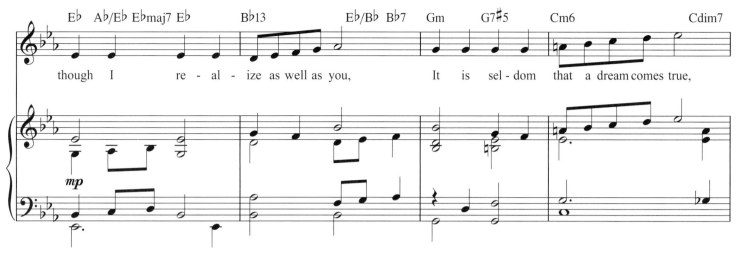

though I re - al - ize as well as you, It is sel - dom that a dream comes true,

Straight 8ths

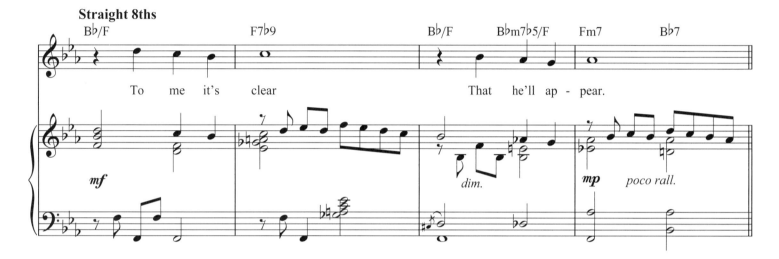

To me it's clear That he'll ap - pear.

Slow Ballad tempo

Some-day he'll come a - long, The man I love; And he'll be big and strong,

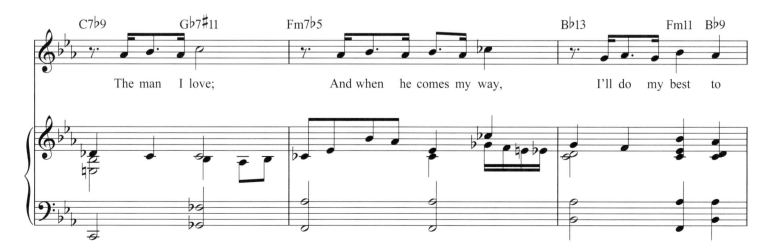

The man I love; And when he comes my way, I'll do my best to

OF THEE I SING

from OF THEE I SING

Music and Lyrics by GEORGE GERSHWIN
and IRA GERSHWIN

From the Is - land of Man - hat - tan to the Coast of

Gold,   From North to South,   From East to West,   You are the love   I love the

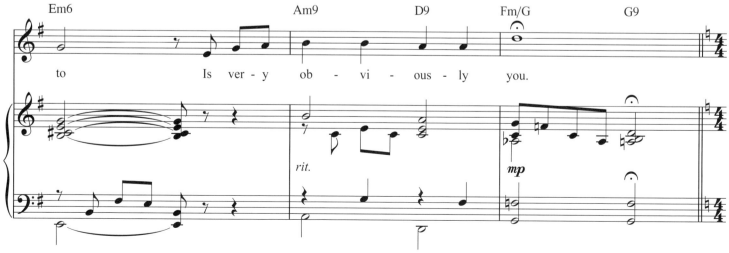

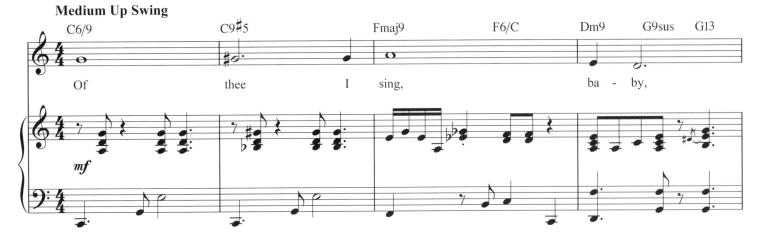

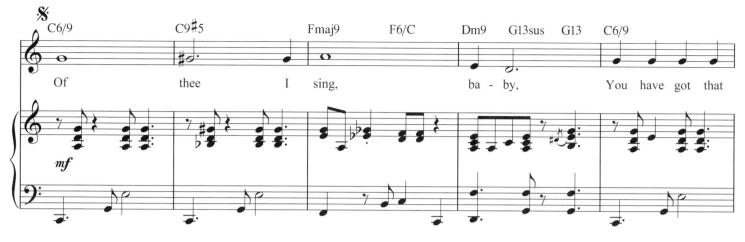

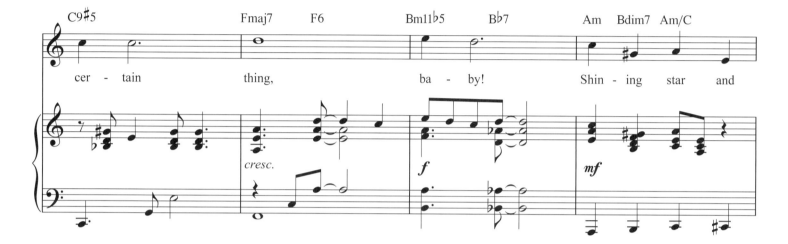

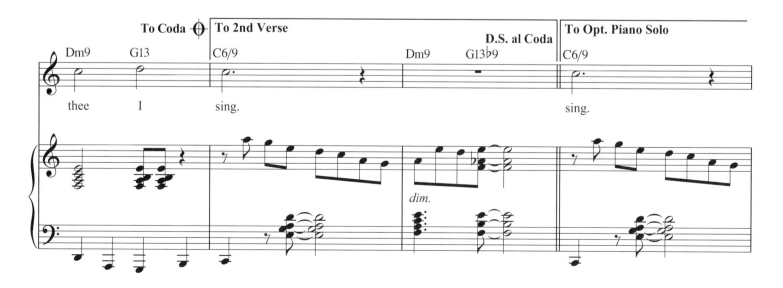

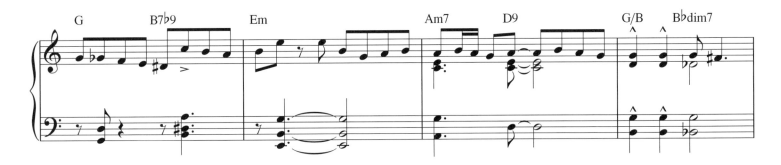

SOMEONE TO WATCH OVER ME

from OH, KAY!

Music and Lyrics by GEORGE GERSHWIN
and IRA GERSHWIN

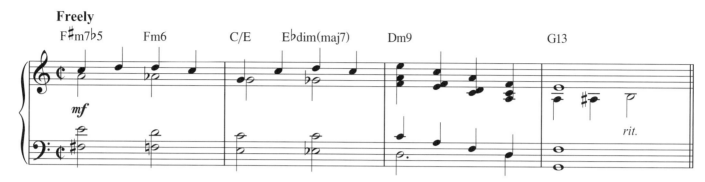

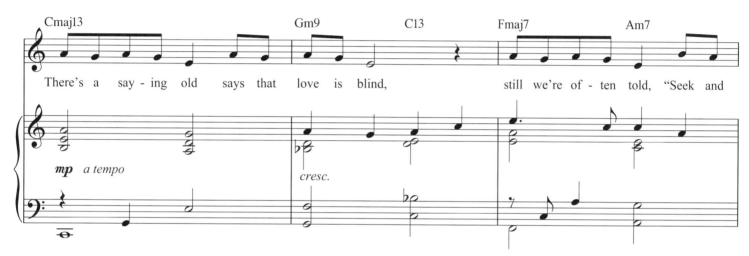

There's a say-ing old says that love is blind, still we're of-ten told, "Seek and

ye shall find." So I'm going to seek a cer-tain lad I've

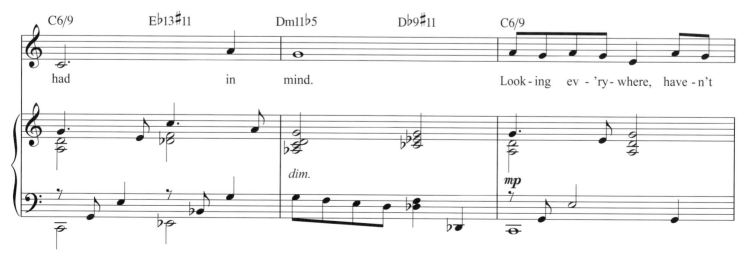

had in mind. Look-ing ev-'ry-where, have-n't

lost in the wood. I know I could al - ways be good

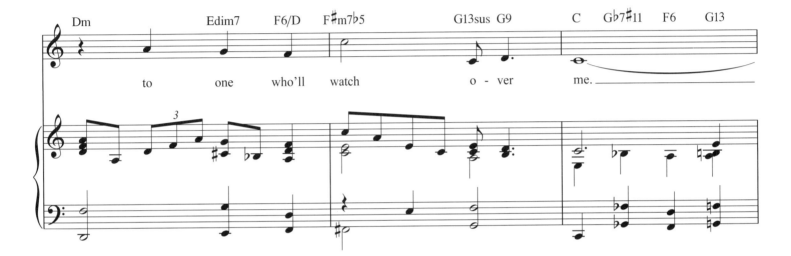

to one who'll watch o - ver me. _____

_____ Al - though he may not be the man some girls

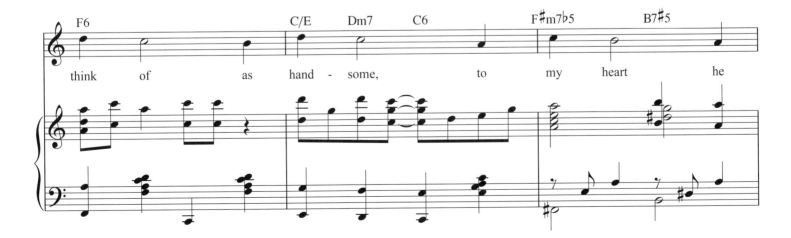

think of as hand - some, to my heart he

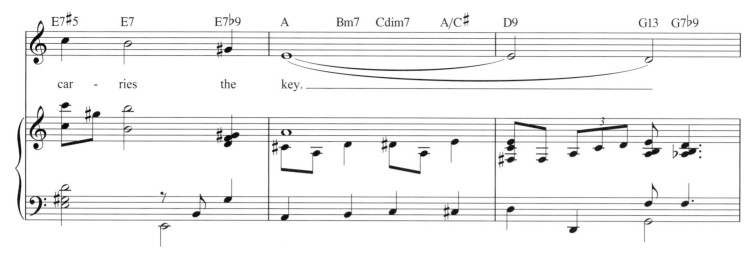

car - ries the key.

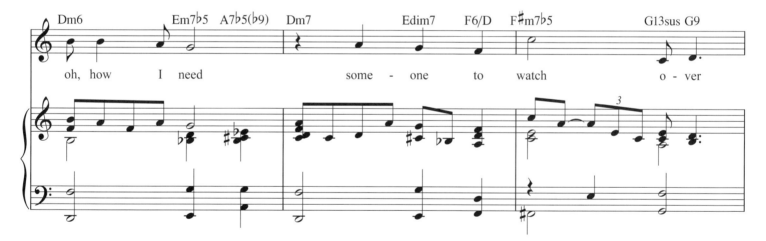

Won't you tell him please to put on some speed, fol - low my lead,

oh, how I need some - one to watch o - ver

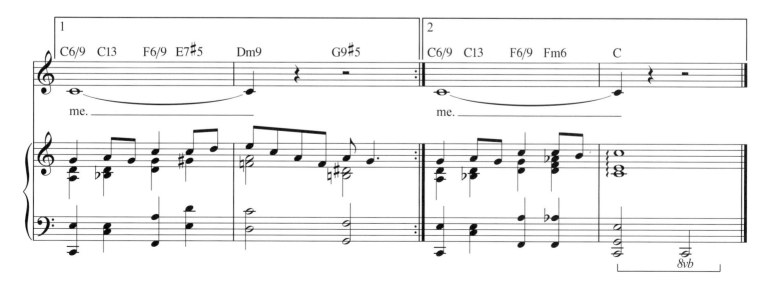

me.

me.

OH, LADY BE GOOD!

from LADY, BE GOOD!

Music and Lyrics by GEORGE GERSHWIN
and IRA GERSHWIN

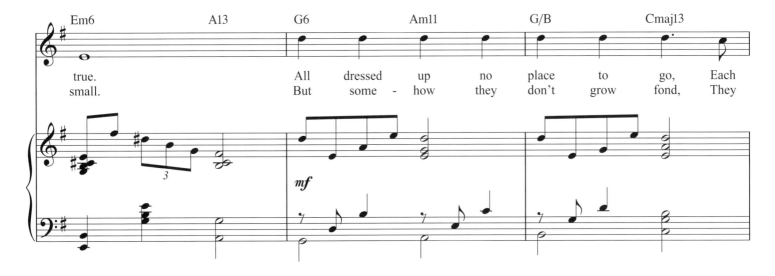

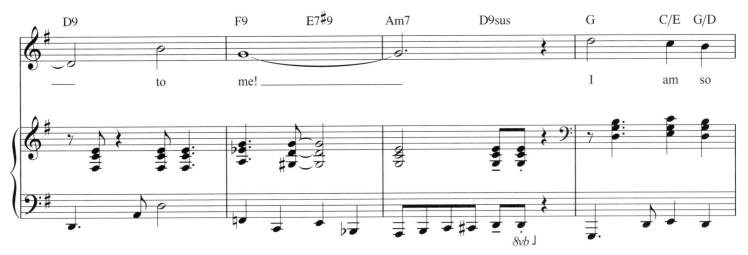

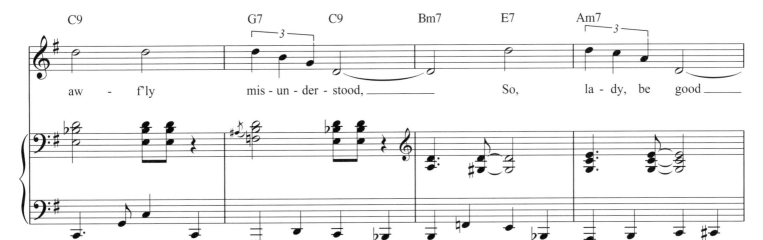

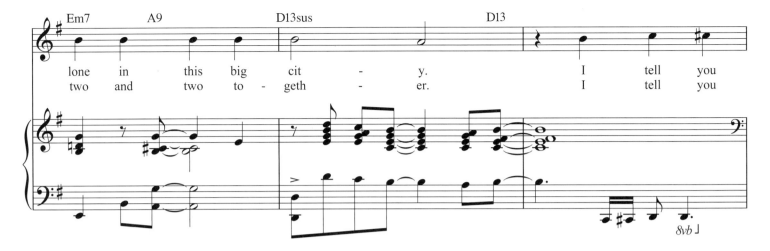

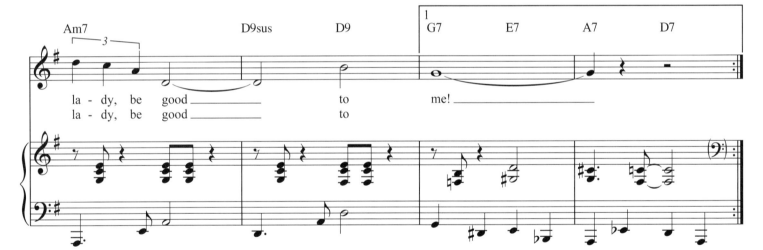

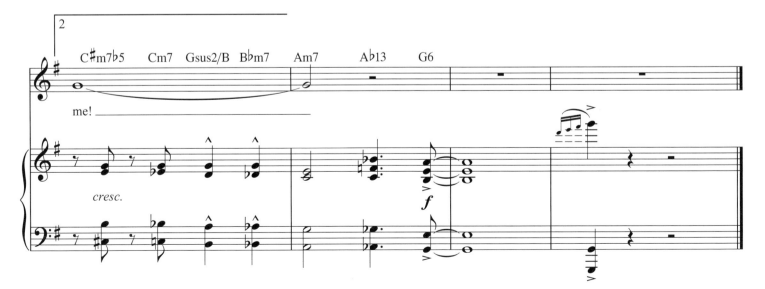

'S WONDERFUL

from FUNNY FACE

Music and Lyrics by GEORGE GERSHWIN
and IRA GERSHWIN

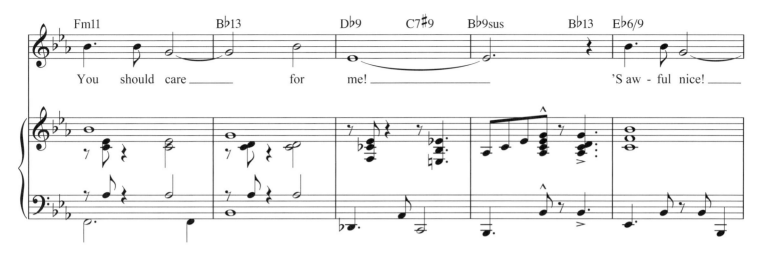

You should care _____ for me! _____ 'S aw - ful nice! _____

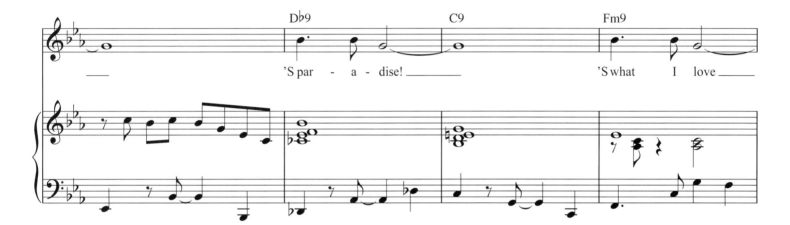

_____ 'S par - a - dise! _____ 'S what I love _____

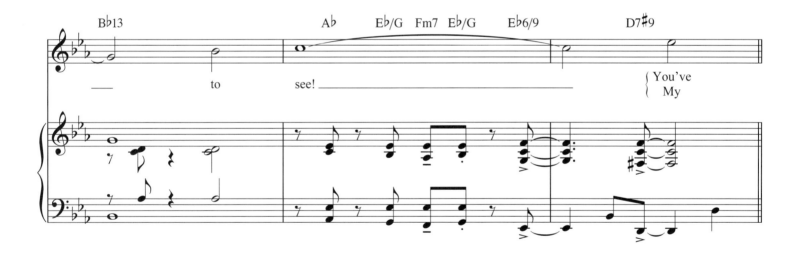

_____ to see! _____ { You've / My

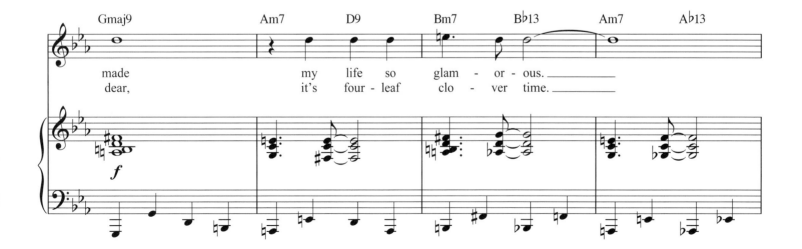

made my life so glam - or - ous. _____
dear, it's four - leaf clo - ver time. _____

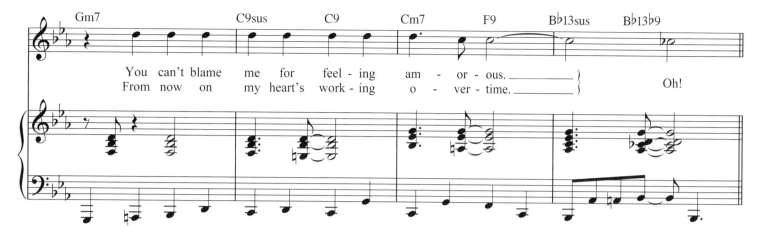

You can't blame me for feel-ing am-or-ous. _____
From now on my heart's work-ing o-ver-time. _____ Oh!

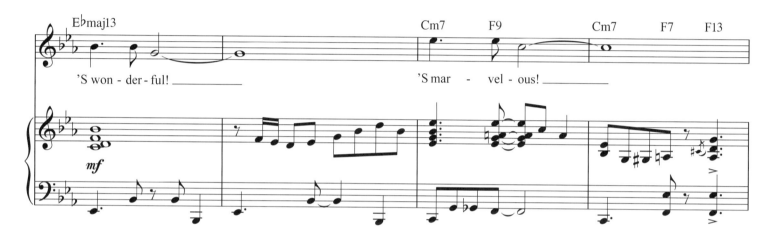

'S won-der-ful! _____ 'S mar - vel-ous! _____

That you should care _____ for me!

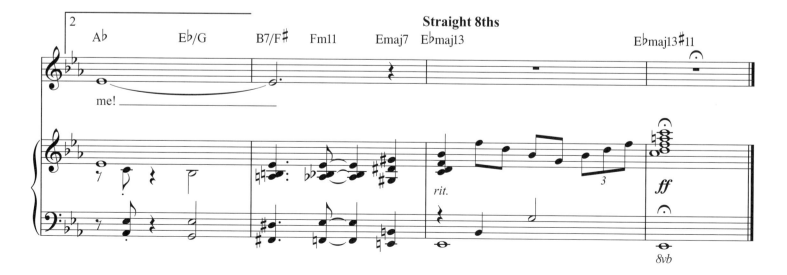

me! _____

Straight 8ths

rit.

ff

8vb

SOMEBODY LOVES ME

from GEORGE WHITE'S SCANDALS OF 1924

Music by GEORGE GERSHWIN
Lyrics by B.G. DeSYLVA
and BALLARD MacDONALD

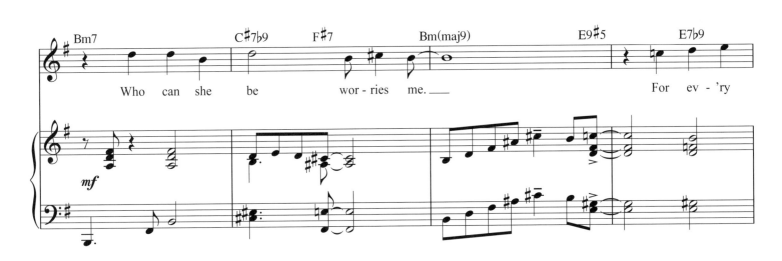

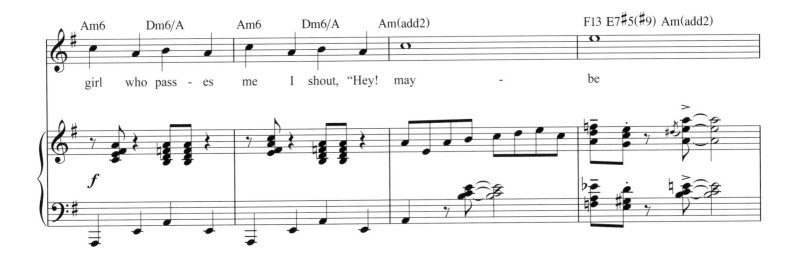

SOON
from STRIKE UP THE BAND

Music and Lyrics by GEORGE GERSHWIN
and IRA GERSHWIN

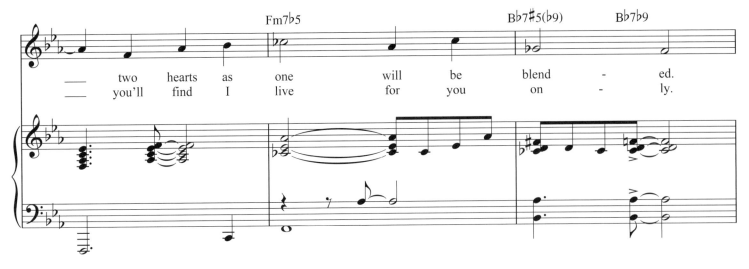

two hearts as one will be blend - ed.
you'll find I live for you on - ly.

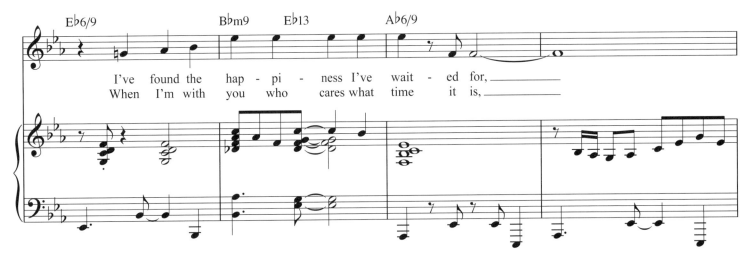

I've found the hap - pi - ness I've wait - ed for, _____
When I'm with you who cares what time it is, _____

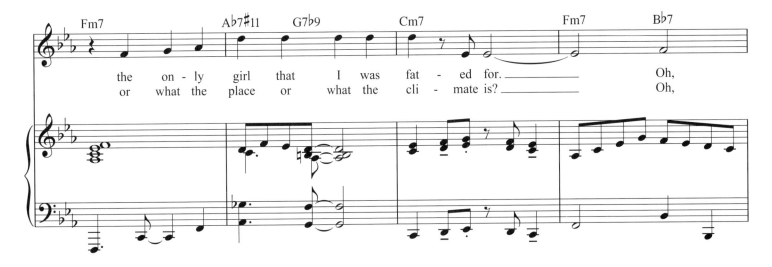

the on - ly girl that I was fat - ed for. _____ Oh,
or what the place or what the cli - mate is? _____ Oh,

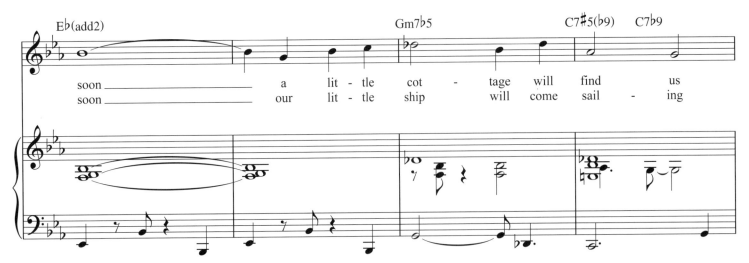

soon _____ a lit - tle cot - tage will find us
soon _____ our lit - tle ship will come sail - ing

SUMMERTIME
from PORGY AND BESS®

Music and Lyrics by GEORGE GERSHWIN,
DuBOSE and DOROTHY HEYWARD
and IRA GERSHWIN

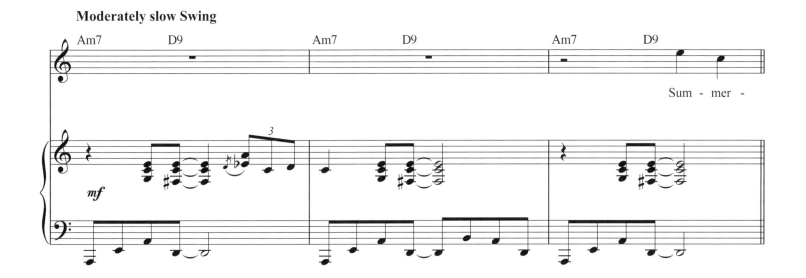

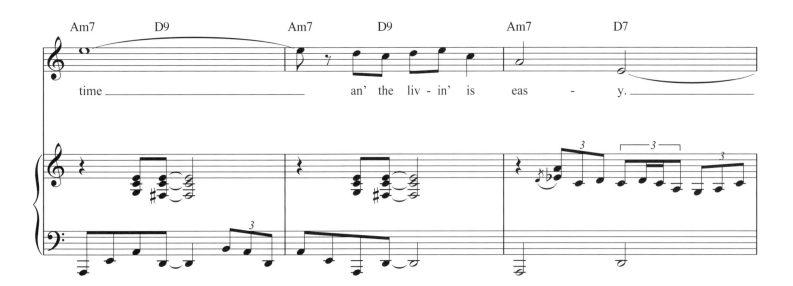

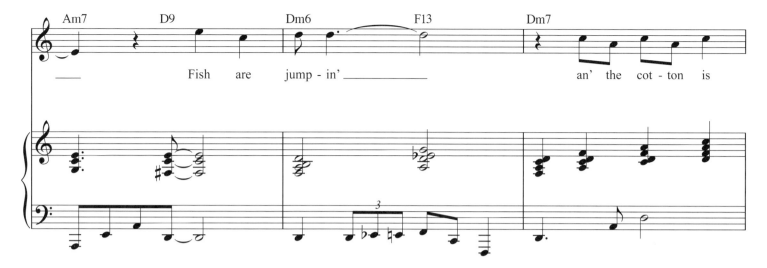

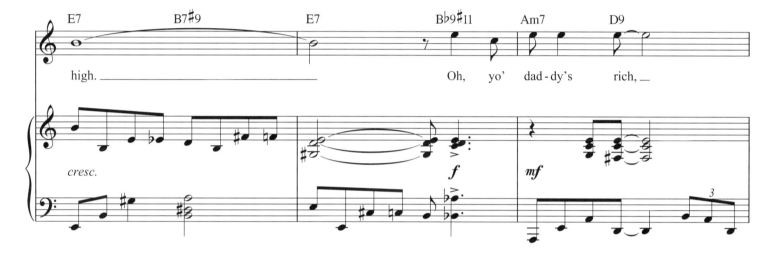

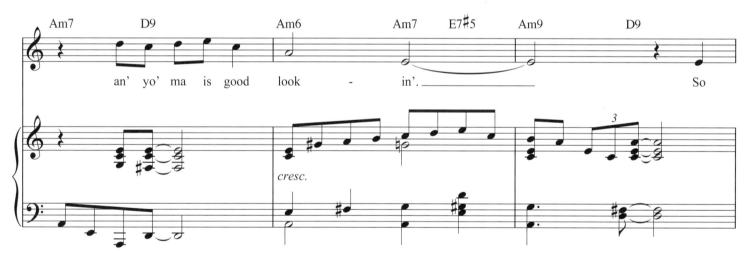

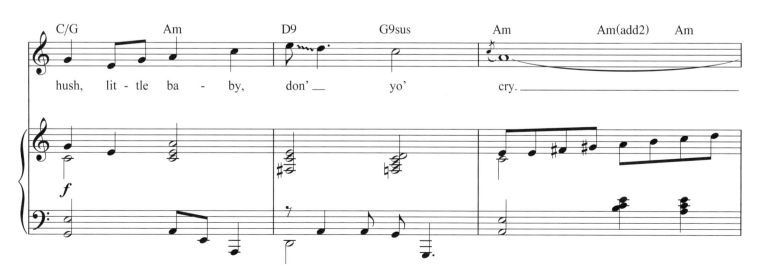

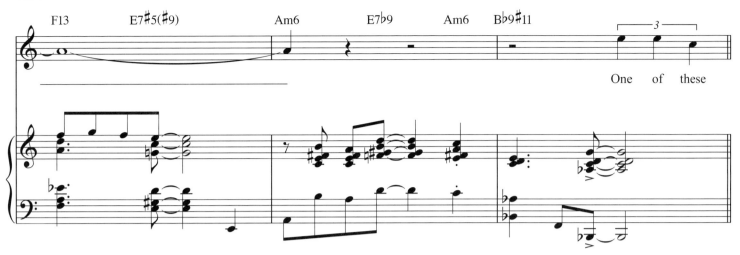

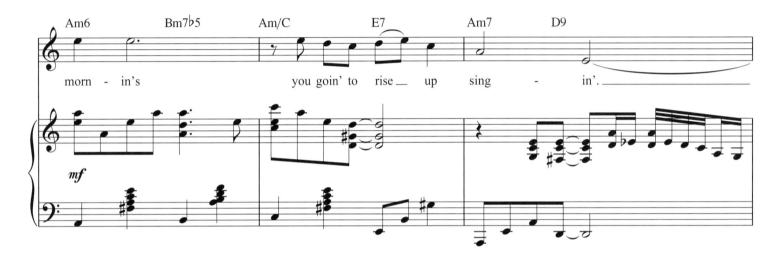

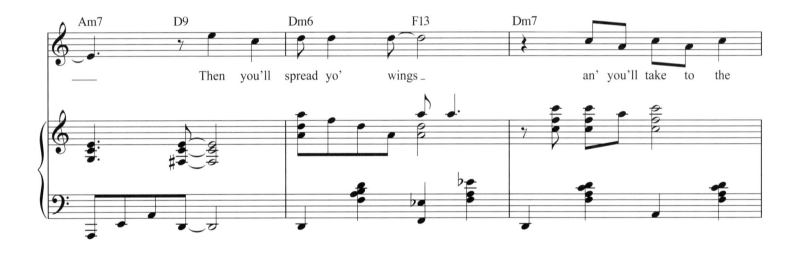

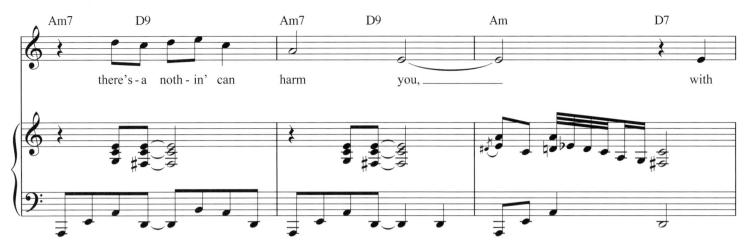

there's-a noth-in' can harm you,_____ with

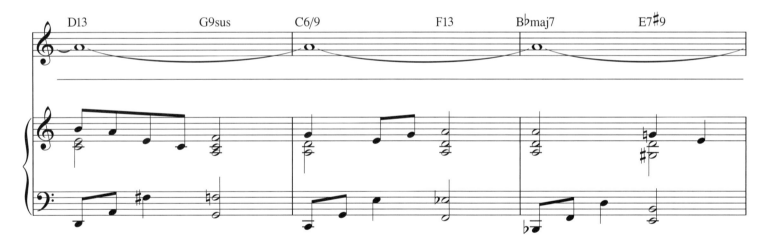

Dad - dy an' Mam - my stand - in' by._____

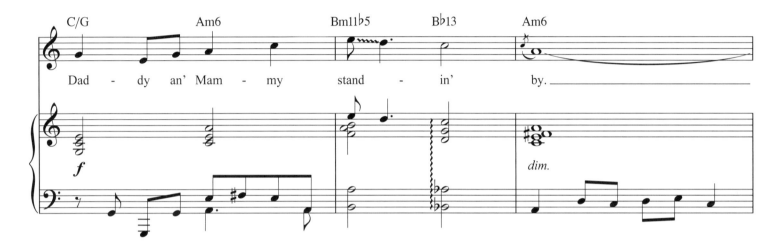

Freely, straight 8ths

THEY ALL LAUGHED
from SHALL WE DANCE

Music and Lyrics by GEORGE GERSHWIN
and IRA GERSHWIN

Light Swing

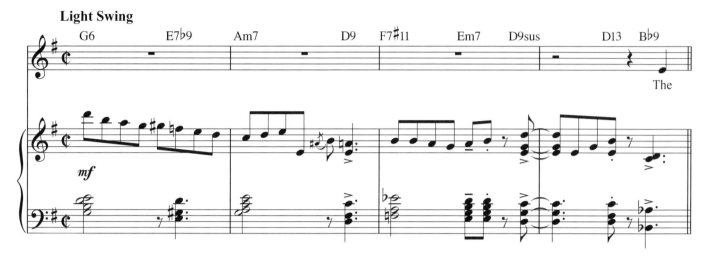

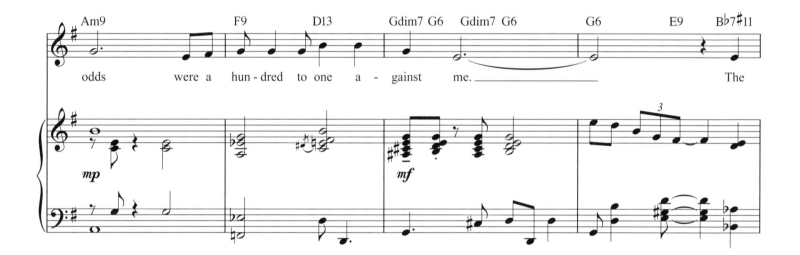

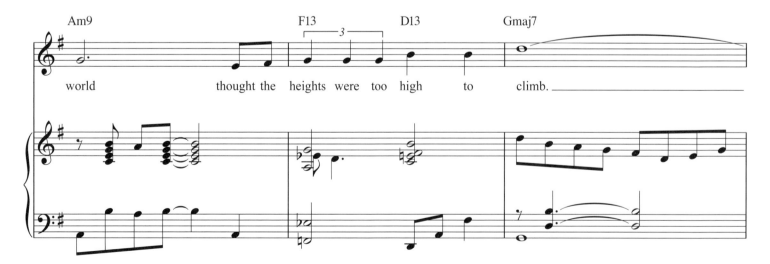

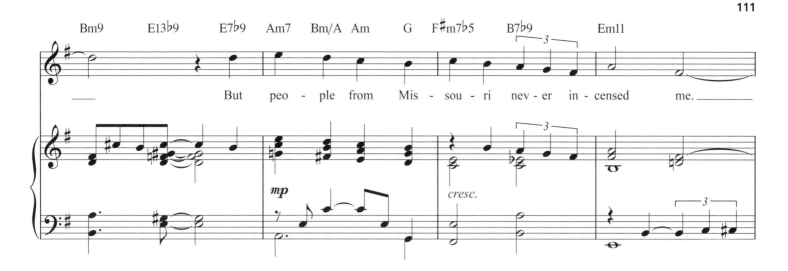

But peo - ple from Mis - sou - ri nev - er in - censed me.

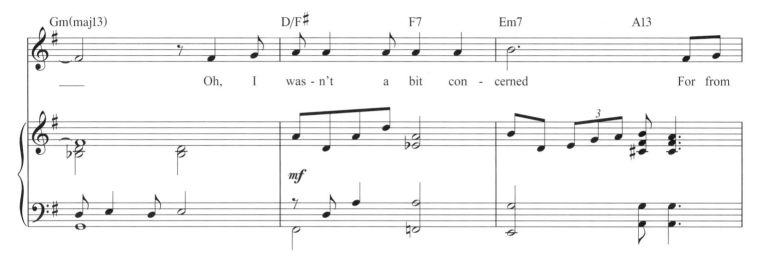

Oh, I was - n't a bit con - cerned For from

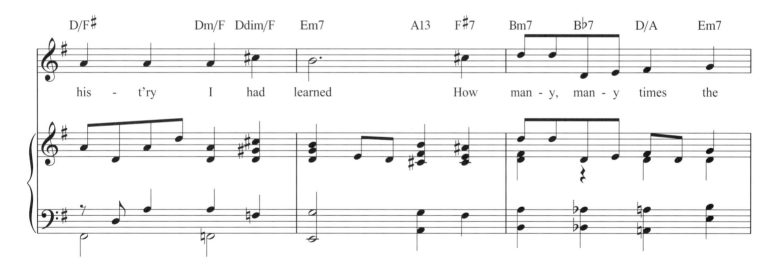

his - t'ry I had learned How man - y, man - y times the

worm had turned.

They told Mar-co-ni wire-less was a pho-ny; it's the same old
Ford and his Liz-zie kept the laugh-ers bus-y; that's how peo-ple

cry. They laughed at me _____ want-ing you, _____ said I was
are. They laughed at me _____ want-ing you, _____ said it would

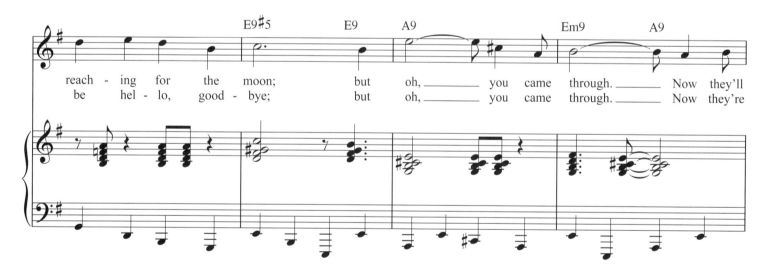

reach-ing for the moon; but oh, _____ you came through. _____ Now they'll
be hel-lo, good-bye; but oh, _____ you came through. _____ Now they're

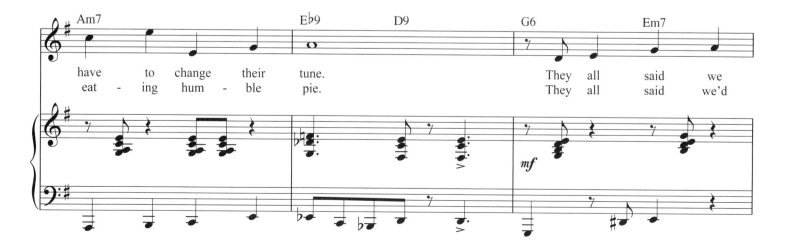

have to change their tune. They all said we
eat-ing hum-ble pie. They all said we'd

THEY CAN'T TAKE THAT AWAY FROM ME

from SHALL WE DANCE

Music and Lyrics by GEORGE GERSHWIN
and IRA GERSHWIN

With movement, straight 8ths

mp

With pedal

rit.

Our ro- mance won't end on a sor- row- ful

mf *a tempo*

note, though by to- mor- row you're gone; the

song is end- ed, but as the song- writ- er wrote, the

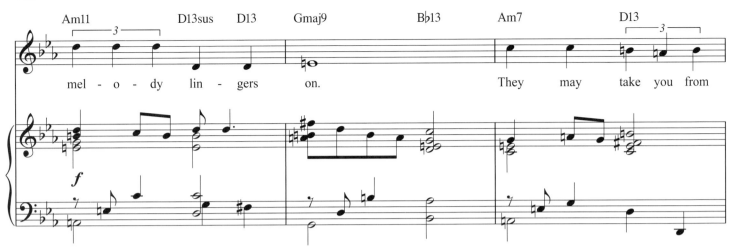

mel - o - dy lin - gers on. They may take you from

me, I'll miss your fond ca - ress. But

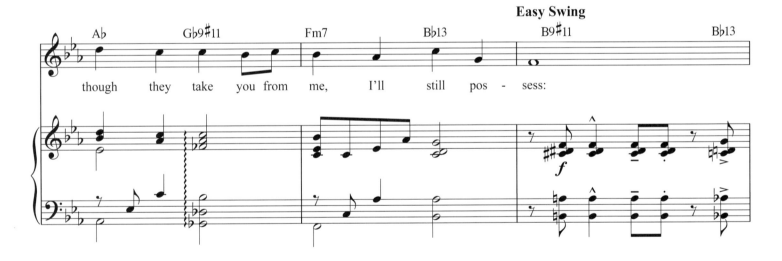

Easy Swing

though they take you from me, I'll still pos - sess:

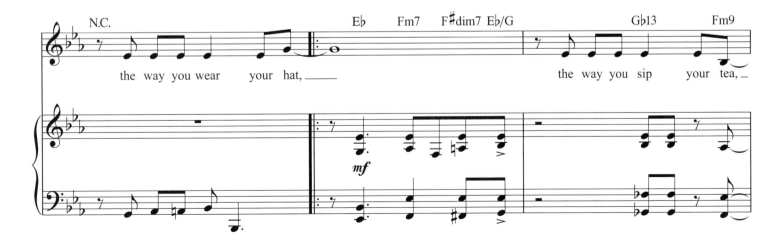

the way you wear your hat, ____ the way you sip your tea, ____

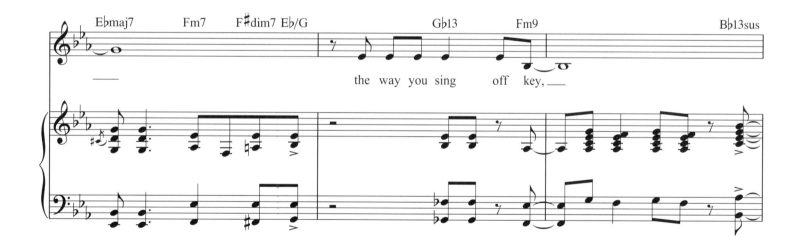

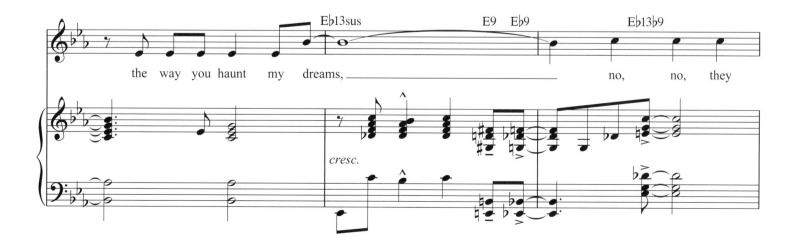

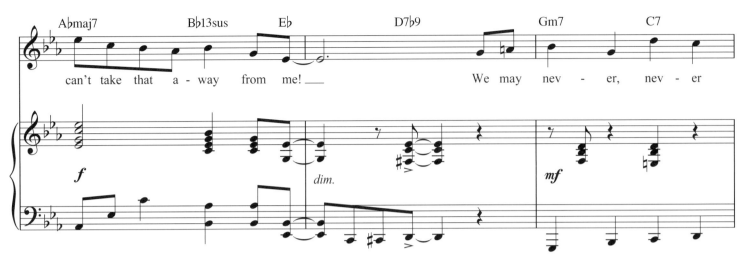

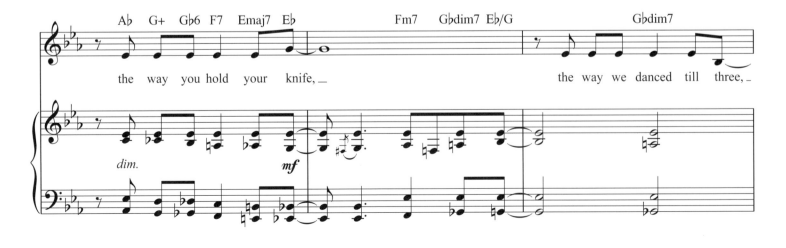

the way you've changed my life.____

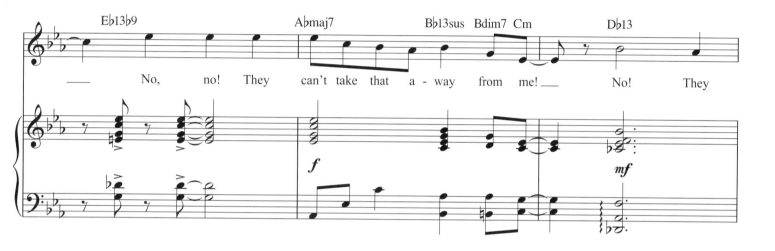

No, no! They can't take that a-way from me!____ No! They

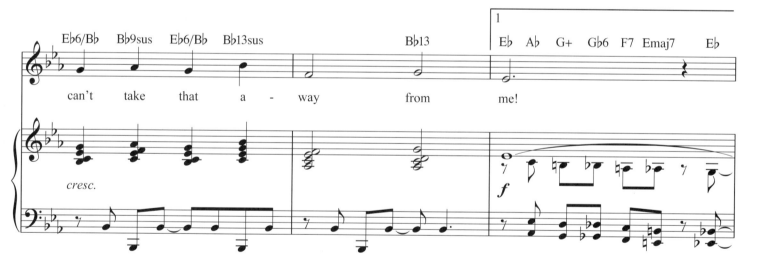

can't take that a - way from me!

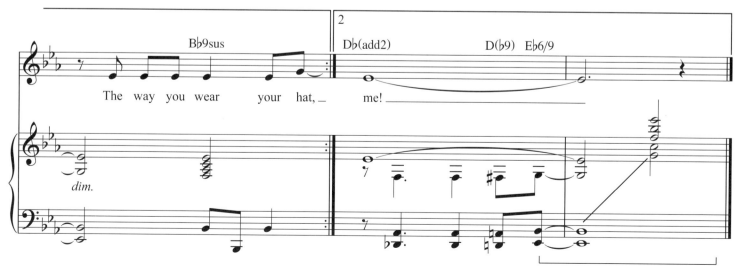

The way you wear your hat, __ me! ____

ORIGINAL KEYS FOR SINGERS

Titles in the Original Keys for Singers series are designed for vocalists looking for authentic transcriptions from their favorite artists. The books transcribe famous vocal performances exactly as recorded and provide piano accompaniment parts so that you can perform or pratice exactly as Ella or Patsy or Josh!

ACROSS THE UNIVERSE

00307010...$19.95

ADELE

00155395...$19.99

LOUIS ARMSTRONG

00307029...$19.99

THE BEATLES

00307400...$19.99

BROADWAY HITS (FEMALE SINGERS)

00119085...$19.99

BROADWAY HITS (MALE SINGERS)

00119084...$19.99

PATSY CLINE

00740072...$22.99

ELLA FITZGERALD

00740252...$22.99

JOSH GROBAN

00306969...$19.99

BILLIE HOLIDAY
Transcribed from Historic Recordings

00740140...$19.99

ETTA JAMES: GREATEST HITS

00130427...$19.99

JAZZ DIVAS

00114959...$19.99

LADIES OF CHRISTMAS

00312192...$19.99

NANCY LAMOTT

00306995...$19.99

MEN OF CHRISTMAS

00312241...$19.99

THE BETTE MIDLER SONGBOOK

00307067...$19.99

THE BEST OF LIZA MINNELLI

00306928...$19.99

ONCE

00102569...$16.99

ELVIS PRESLEY

00138200...$19.99

SHOWSTOPPERS FOR FEMALE SINGERS

00119640...$19.99

BEST OF NINA SIMONE

00121576...$19.99

FRANK SINATRA – MORE OF HIS BEST

00307081...$19.99

TAYLOR SWIFT

00142702...$16.99

SARAH VAUGHAN

00306558...$24.99

VOCAL POP

00312656 ....$19.99

ANDY WILLIAMS – CHRISTMAS COLLECTION

00307158...$17.99

ANDY WILLIAMS

00307160...$17.99

HAL•LEONARD®
www.halleonard.com

Prices, contents, and availability subject to change without notice.